The Cowal \
in Argyll

CONTENTS

**EXPLANATION OF TEXT
ABBREVIATIONS IN ROUTE
DESCRIPTIONS:**
R: Right, L: Left,
N: North, S: South,
E: East, W: West.

Introduction to this Book

This guide describes, in six day-by-day sections, a continuous walk across the Cowal Peninsula - plus seven additional 'loop walks' on the way. The main 'spine' could occupy a week-long holiday or, with added loops, up to a fortnight. Alternatively, individual walks can be selected as 'one offs' by resident and visitor alike.

The guide begins with brief introductions to the way and the Cowal Peninsula, followed by a summary of each of the thirteen walks. Its core consists of a map and a detailed route description for each walk. In addition there is a section describing places and themes of heritage and environmental interest along or near to the spine of the way.

To help you to assess your preparedness, the degree of difficulty of each walk is defined on a scale of 1 to 10. Those graded 3 or less (spine sections 3 and 4 and loop walks 3 and 4) are on road or a good track surface throughout and are very suitable for anyone who wants a one-off walk avoiding rough country (though they may still come across steep ascents). Those graded 7 or more (spine sections 2, 5 and 6; loop walks 5 and 6) contain at least one long, remote section of rough or hard going. Loop walk 1 (grade 5) makes a good, not over-long introduction to rough going for walkers with little experience.

Anyone aiming to complete the whole way should therefore have some walking experience, but not necessarily of a long-distance way.

If you've never tried a multi-day walk before, you'll find the Cowal Way a good introduction, being neither too long overall nor having any excessively long days. Cowal is big enough, nevertheless, to give you a sense of achievement and its peninsular nature lends a pleasing natural unity to the walk.

Preparedness for whatever the weather might bring is important. Cowal shares the climate of the rest of the west highlands, which means that extremes of heat and cold aren't common, but wind and wet are. These, in combination with height and / or exposure, can produce a wind chill that will make the effective temperature that you experience very much lower than the air temperature. Your clothing and equipment must be sufficient to cope whatever the season. Good and bad weather can be experienced here at any time of year, so no guarantees. Check forecasts, and be prepared for rapid variation in the day's weather.

The route descriptions and maps within the book should be used in conjunction with the appropriate Ordnance Survey 1 : 25 000 ('Pathfinder') maps.

Introduction to the Cowal Way

The Cowal Way, conceived by Jim McLuckie of Colintraive and Glendaruel Community Council, is a mini long distance footpath running the length of the Cowal Peninsula. It starts in the SW at Portavadie, beside Loch Fyne, and finishes in the NE at Ardgartan, by Loch Long. It is 75.2 km (47 miles) long, climbing 1540m (5050 feet) on the way.

The way and its loop walks follow existing rights of way and public roads, most of which are extremely quiet, or cross Forestry Commission land, which includes a good deal of open hill. Access is not an issue, but don't expect the line to be waymarked everywhere; the route descriptions should always be read with care.

The 'spine' of the way is divided into six sections of varying length and difficulty. Fit walkers will certainly be able to cover the distance in less than six days if they want to, which is fine, but the intention has been to plan a route that can be enjoyed slowly. Accordingly, the way takes in, and the guide book refers to, many places and themes of 'heritage interest' which you might like to explore. ('Heritage' has been defined widely to include natural and scenic as well as historical and cultural heritage).

In addition to the six sections that make up the 'spine' of the way, there are seven 'loop' walks, each of which starts and finishes near an overnight stop. A potential exception is the walk from Tighnabruaich to Kilfinan, which is not a true loop, but an 'out and back', where walkers might like to consider arranging transport back to Tighnabruaich. For those doing the full length of the way, a selection of these loop walks can be a means of extending your exploration and enjoyment of Cowal. Alternatively, they can be taken as one-off 'day walks'.

The length and height gain is given for each walk, together with a brief indication as to its degree of difficulty and the time it might take. This is partly a subjective exercise, so approach with caution and always read the detailed route descriptions so that you'll be aware of any particular hazards or difficulties associated with a particular walk.

Accommodation is not plentiful close to the start and finish of the way (unless you are camping or, in the case of the finish, youth hostelling), but can be found not too far away at Tighnabruaich and Arrochar respectively. En route, most awkward in this respect are the north end of Glendaruel (bus or taxi may be necessary) and Glenbranter (where there is the option of walking on to Strachur).

Introduction to the Area

Cowal is part of Argyll, in the SW of the Scottish Highlands. Paradoxically, at one and the same time it's very accessible yet very little known. Despite its barriers of sea and hill, this is especially surprising because there is so much to recommend it - beauty, great peace and wildness, together with a long and fascinating history.

Reputedly named from Comhgal, a prince of the Gaels, the peninsula lies moated between Loch Fyne to the west and Loch Long and the Firth of Clyde to the east. To the south it divides into three 'prongs', while to the north its boundary is the belt of mountains between the heads of Loch Long and Loch Fyne. It's about 50km long, and between 12 and 25km wide. Access by road is via the A82 from Glasgow, the A83 over the Rest and be Thankful pass and the A815. Car ferries run to Dunoon from Gourock; to Portavadie, in the SW, from Tarbert (Loch Fyne); and from the Isle of Bute to Colintraive in the S. Fewer than 20,000 people live here, most of them, in or near Dunoon.

Cowal is geologically highland. Its dominant rocks are hard, ancient metamorphic schists; grey, but shot through with white quartz veins. Only in the south-east, at Toward, do lowland sandstones have a

toehold where the highland faultline clips Argyll.

The land is hilly and divided by deep glens and narrow sea lochs or fiords. Apart from the south-western Ardlamont 'prong' and around Dunoon, only the glen floors and the equally narrow, often steep and rocky, coastal strips are below 200m. The high ground divides into two; around and north-east of Loch Eck it is especially mountainous and rugged, with many tops above 600m, while the hills of the southern and western fringes are lower and, for the most part, more rounded.

Wild country means wild animals, so keep your eyes open to earth, sea and sky as you go. Red deer and common seal are likely at some point in your walk, while roe deer and otter are more elusive. Amongst birds, Cowal has at least three pairs of golden eagle, and there are peregrine falcon, hen harrier, and lots of buzzards, to name a few of the more spectacular species. By the sea you'll come across eider and merganser, there's no lack of woodland birds, and, these days, our grassy hills of spring and summer are better than most places for the skylark.

Mountains plus western location give a mild, moist climate. With these conditions, and given our acid rocks, peaty or leached acid soils naturally support oak-birch woodland. Attractive fragments lie along our route, with their characteristic associates such as rowan, the traditional foiler of witchcraft. Beneath the trees, in spring, expect flowers such as wood anemone, wood sorrel, wild garlic, primrose and violet. In season, the Lauder walks at Glenbranter are excellent for bluebells, while everywhere and at all times there are soft cushions of moss, and abundant lichens testify to clean air.

On grassy hill or heathery moorland typical flowers include tormentil, milkwort, bog asphodel and heath spotted orchid, as well as the carnivorous sundew and butterwort. The beautiful delicately-veined white flower of grass of Parnassus can be found in richer, flushed patches of soil.

Comhgal, a Gaelic-speaking Iron Age Scot, was part of the colonisation of Argyll from Ireland, but his people were by no means the first here. From as long ago as 6000 years, Stone Age and Bronze Age predecessors left their enduring marks on Cowal in the form of standing stones, burial cairns, rock carvings and hut traces. SW Cowal, in particular, must have been quite densely-populated in prehistoric times.

Comhgal's Iron Age must have been turbulent, as what remains now is mostly fortification; duns or bigger hill forts. From earliest historic times, however, we find the remnants of several early christian chapels, impressive for the feelings they and their surroundings can evoke rather than for the extent of the ruins themselves. Medieval

times also brought castles, such as the Lamonts' ruined Asgog, and some fine celtic-patterned grave slabs in or near the churches at Kilfinan, Glendaruel and Strachur.

Cowal's traditional livelihood has been from farming, as witnessed by the ruins of abandoned townships with their associated traces of cultivation. Nor have today's farmers, with their focus on sheep or beef cattle, had it easy in recent years. Apart from pasture, few crops can be grown other than roots for fodder or grass for silage, though there are exceptions in areas of better ground, for example in Glendaruel and in the SW. Fish farming has become very important along Loch Fyne and in Loch Riddon in recent years.

The greatest alteration in Cowal's landscape during the twentieth century, though, has been the establishment of extensive forest plantations. Although initially uniform in appearance, differential felling over time produces a mosaic effect and access along forest roads is a useful secondary benefit.

Cowal has several villages, but, away from Dunoon, only Lochgoilhead, Strachur and Tighnabruaich/Kames are of any size. Elsewhere, services, including public transport, are limited enough to make planning ahead worthwhile. See the notes with each spine section.

Tourist information offices in Cowal: Dunoon (01369) 703785; Ardgartan (01301) 702432.

Summary of the Spine Walk

■ **Section 1** **Portavadie to Tighnabruaich.** We begin with a very varied walk through the land of the Lamonts. Starting and finishing by sea lochs, it traverses planted forests, the shores of a lochan by a ruined castle, green pastures, a small village with a ruined gunpowder works, a golf course(!) and broadleaved woods. Oh, and there are magnificent views of Arran, Tighnabruaich and the Kyles of Bute. Practically the whole of Cowal in miniature!

The going is varied, too. There are forest roads, quiet stretches of public road, and a lot of path - some clear and good, some better described as trods. There are also a few short pathless stretches, but no really big climbs; instead the route as a whole is gently undulating. Take your time, and enjoy it.

■ **Section 2** **Tighnabruaich to Glendaruel.** Beginning as a glorious coastal walk beside the Kyles of Bute and Loch Riddon, today's route continues along public roads into quiet Glendaruel. Quitting the Victorian splendour of Tighnabruaich's villas and gardens, our route north is initially along easy forest roads, with sea birds and scenery for company. Beyond Glen Caladh there is a much rougher stretch beside the shore,

then up through dense woodland to Craig Lodge. It's not very far, but do allow plenty of time for this section, especially if you have a heavy pack and the tide's in. An hour is not too much. Take a breather by Craig Lodge - the view from the pier is good and you deserve it. From here on, the route is mostly flat and on roads, but compensated by the surrounding woods and waters, fields and hills. Take care at the broken bridge beyond Waulkmill.

■ **Section 3** **Glendaruel.** To-day's walk is best taken slowly to savour the peace and quiet of this ancient glen. The distance is not great, and there is virtually no climb. Having time, then, before you leave the Clachan, Kilmodan church and the collection of late-medieval carved graveslabs in their churchyard building, are well worth a tiny detour. When ready to set out, our route lies along the west glen road, a delightful backwater.... but Glendaruel is the kind of place where even the main road is not very busy.

It's as well to be aware that there is little accommodation near the north end of Glendaruel. Unless you want to continue to Glenbranter and Strachur (a long way), it's worth checking current bus timetables or taxis the previous day to be sure of getting back to stay at Clachan, elsewhere in Glendaruel, or even at Tighnabruaich (and out again next morning, if continuing).

■ **Section 4 Glendaruel to Glenbranter.** To-day you'll probably see very few people, if any at all, between the farm at Garvie and the first houses at Glenbranter, as you cross a remote pass. The walking is easy underfoot, being on forest tracks throughout once beyond Garvie. On the way up, from open ground, there are good views to Creag Tharsuinn's high ridge and back to Glendaruel. Once much beyond the dam and into the forest, a stony burn is frequently seen burbling away attractively (and sometimes accessibly) on your left, with a stretch of rapids and mini-falls by Point 9. Having crossed the pass, the steep, rugged mountains around Loch Eck come into view from lower down Glen Branter. If you're early enough, think about going round the loop of the Lauder walk from Point 15 - it's a lovely wooded gorge.

■ **Section 5 Glenbranter to Lochgoilhead.** Now we're really into mountain country, crossing a wild pass between high hills. There is some beautiful wild landscape on the way, especially beyond the summit of the Bealach an Lochain, notably a hill loch, enormous rockfalls, a rocky burn with a really superb waterfall and great views over Loch Goil. But first a gently pastoral walk on peaceful back roads takes us from Glenbranter to Strachur and on towards Succoth Farm. After this, forest roads take us steeply, but otherwise easily, almost to the summit of our pass. Now comes the really hard stuff.

Over the bealach, beside Curra Lochan and down its burn there is much tussock and bog, only intermittently threaded by sketchy path, before a last forest track leads more easily down to Loch Goil and the road to Lochgoilhead. Take things slowly and enjoy the scenery. River crossings can occasionally give difficulty on this section: read the route description carefully.

■ **Section 6 Lochgoilhead to Ardgartan.** A day surrounded by big mountains and spectacular scenery. The Cobbler's 'shark's fin' of a South Peak is a feature of the ascent away to our left, and, as we reach the summit of a high pass, the views back include far away island hills. Ahead Ben Lomond makes an elegant cone. Oddly, we are in countryside once wholly owned by the City of Glasgow! From 1905 to 1965, the city used these Ardgoil hills, gifted to it by Lord Rowallan, for the benefit of all of its citizens, and they are still very much a playground and 'lung' for Clydesiders.

Big mountains, then, and a higher pass than the Bealach an Lochain, but easier going underfoot. There is always some trodden line at the very least, few tussocks, and much of our way is on track or well-made path. At the end of the day, there is a stretch of lightly-used tarmac beside Loch Long.

You've completed your walk across Cowal; how about climbing the Cobbler tomorrow as a fitting climax?

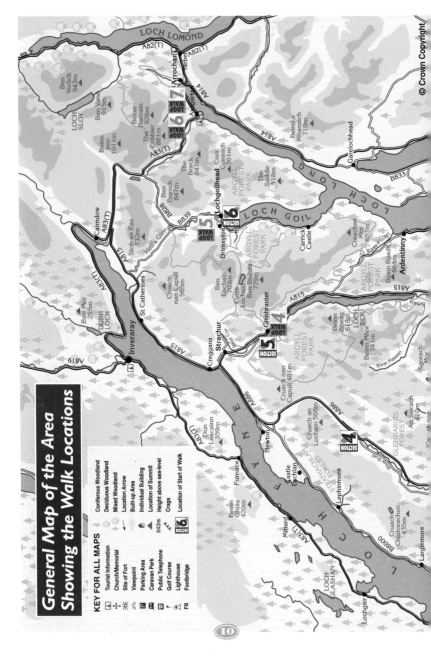

General Map of the Area
Showing the Walk Locations

KEY FOR ALL MAPS

- **i** Tourist Information
- **†** Church/Memorial
- **※** Site of Fort
- **※** Viewpoint
- **P** Parking Area
- **C** Caravan Park
- **☎** Public Telephone
- **⚲** Golf Course
- **★** Lighthouse
- **FB** Footbridge

- Coniferous Woodland
- Deciduous Woodland
- Mixed Woodland
- ↓ Location Arrow
- Built-up Area
- Individual Building
- ▲ Location of Summit
- 643m Height above sea-level
- Crags
- **SECTION 6** Location of Start of Walk

© Crown Copyright

LOCH LOMOND

Ben Vorlich 943m

LOCH SLOY

Ben Vane 915m

Beinn Narnain 926m The Cobbler 881m

Beinn Ime 1011m

Arrochar

Tarbet

A82(T)

A82(T)

A83(T)

A814

LOOP WALK 6

LOOP WALK 7

Ardgartan

Cairndow

A83(T)

B828

B839

Stob an Eas 732m

Hell's Glen

The Brack 847m

Cnoc Coinnich 761m

Ben Donich 847m

LOOP WALK 5

Lochgoilhead

Drimsynie

SECTION 6

The Saddle 518m

ARGYLL FOREST PARK

LOCH GOIL

Benn a' Mhanaich 710m

Garelochhead

B833

LOCH LONG

St Catherines

DUBH LOCH

A819

Inveraray

i

Cruach nan Capull 560m

Ben Lochain 703m

Curra Lochain

Ben Bheula 779m

ARGYLL FOREST PARK

Carrick Castle

Creachan Mor 657m

Ardentinny

River Finart

Benn Reudle 664m

ARGYLL FOREST PARK

A815

Beinn Mor 255m

Ceggans

Strachur

Beinn Bheag 619m

LOCH ECK

Beinn Mhor 741m

River Massan

Sgeodh

An Scrcoh 410m

Glenbranter

LOOP WALK 4

SECTION 5

ARGYLL FOREST PARK

A815

A886

Black Cut

LOCH FYNE

Cruach nan Capull 481m

Dun Leacainn 399m

Newton

Furnace

Cruach an Lochain 508m

STRACHACHLAN FOREST

Lephinmore

SECTION 4

A886

B8000

GLENDARUEL FOREST

An Sgorach 410m

Beinn Ghlas 420m

Castle Lachlan

Minard

A83(T)

Cruach Chuileachan 435m

Largiemore

LOCH GLASHAN

Lochgair

10

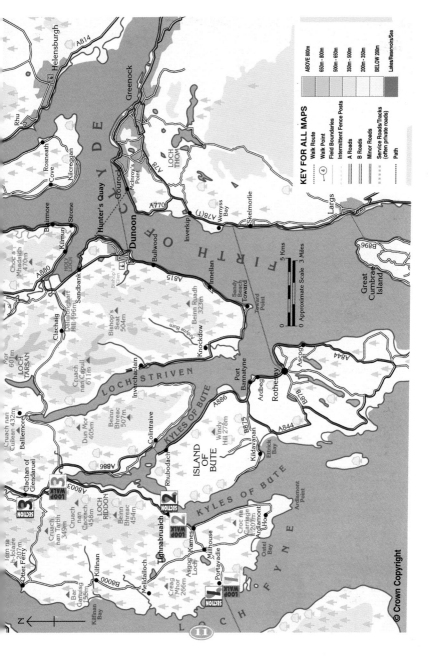

KEY FOR ALL MAPS

—❸— Walk Route
⊕ Walk Point
Field Boundaries
Intermittent Fence Posts
A Roads
B Roads
Minor Roads
Service Roads/Tracks (often private roads)
Path

ABOVE 800m
650m - 800m
500m - 650m
350m - 500m
200m - 350m
BELOW 200m
Lakes/Reservoirs/Sea

Helensburgh
A814
Rhu
Rosneath
Cove
Kilcreggan
Greenock
FIRTH OF CLYDE
McInroy's Point
Gourock
LOCH THOM
Blairmore
Strone
Kilmun
A880
HOLY LOCH
Hunter's Quay
Dunoon
A770
Wemyss Bay
Inverkip
Skelmorlie
A78(T)
Largs
Choc a Mhadaidh 470m
Sandbank
Bishop's Seat 504m
Bullwood
A815
Innellan
Clachaig
Ballochgair Hill 196m
LOCH TARSAN
Mor 601m
Cruach nan Capull 611m
Benn Ruadh 323m
Knockdow
Sandy Beach Toward
Toward Point
Great Cumbrae Island
B896
Cruach nan Cuilean 432m
Balliemore
Inverchaolain
LOCH STRIVEN
Dun Mor 405m
Benn Bhreac 507m
Colintraive
KYLES OF BUTE
A886
Port Bannatyne
Ardbeg
Rothesay
A844
Ascog
A844
Windy Hill 278m
B875
Kildavanan
B878
Iorn na h-Iolaire 207m
Otter Ferry
Clachan of Glendaruel
SECTION 3
WALK 3 LOOP
A8003
Cruach nan Tarbh 349m
Cruach nan Caorach 456m
LOCH RIDDON
Benn Bhreac 454m
Rhubodach
ISLAND OF BUTE
Etrick Bay
KYLES OF BUTE
Ardmont Point
Kilfinan
B8000
Melldalloch
Tighnabruaich
SECTION 2
WALK 2 LOOP
Kames
Millhouse
Croc na Carraige 210m
Ardlamont Ho.
Ostel Bay
Bar Garuisg 155m
Kilfinan Bay
Creag 'Mhor 266m
Ascog Loch
Portavadie
SECTION 1
WALK 1 LOOP
LOCH FYNE

0 5 Kms
0 Approximate Scale 3 Miles

N

11

© Crown Copyright

PORTAVADIE - TIGHNABRUAICH
10km (6.3 miles)

Route Details

Distance	10km (6.3 miles)
Degree of Difficulty	Easy to Moderate
Ascent	180m (590ft)
Time	5 hours

Start and Finish Points

Start: Portavadie, at the Forestry Commission's Glenan Walk car park (GR 928698). 'Wee Geoff's Buses' run to Portavadie (Tarbert ferry) from Dunoon (4 days/week) and Tighnabruaich. Tel. 01700 811473. Stagecoach Western Buses (01369 707701) run to Portavadie from Dunoon twice weekly. Taxis (all 01700 nos.) from M. Critchley (811425/811392); P. McBride (811877/811660) and G. MacLellan (811441). Finish: Tighnabruaich (PO & shops & hotel) at GR 979728. Transport tels. above & Section 2.

Maps Needed

OS Pathfinder No. 400 (NR 87/97)
OS Landranger No. 62

Parking Facilities

Portavadie at GR 928698.
Tighnabruaich at GR 983731.

Route Description

■ **1** Turn L onto the concrete road. Follow it uphill for 250m.

■ **2** Turn L onto a forest road (opposite a half-hidden sign; 'path to Ascog' (sic). Follow it for 700m until a sharp (90°) L turn is reached just before passing under an electricity line.

■ **3** Turn R at the 90° corner onto a path briefly surfaced with reddish stones. There is a crude 'path to Ascog' (sic) sign and a paint splashed wooden marker post (more posts between here and Loch Asgog). Follow the grassy path (high bracken) for 100m.

■ **4** Emerge into a clearing (three houses + older ruins). Skirt the near edge of the clearing to the R (marker post) to go gently uphill (tall conifers on R). Within 200m the path steepens, then turns R to reach a summit level.

■ **5** The path descends SE to cross a wide clearing, passes through a screen of conifers, crosses a second large clearing, swings L and descends steeply to cross a gully and fence line between orange-painted iron gate posts (250m). About 40m beyond the fence it enters a clearly-defined forest ride which it follows, through occasional clearings, to Loch Asgog (500m).

■ **6** Loch Asgog is seen across a clearing. Follow the path along the L edge of the clearing until directly above Asgog castle and cottages, then turn to descend towards the shore.

■ **7** Just by the castle, the path joins the track serving the cottages.

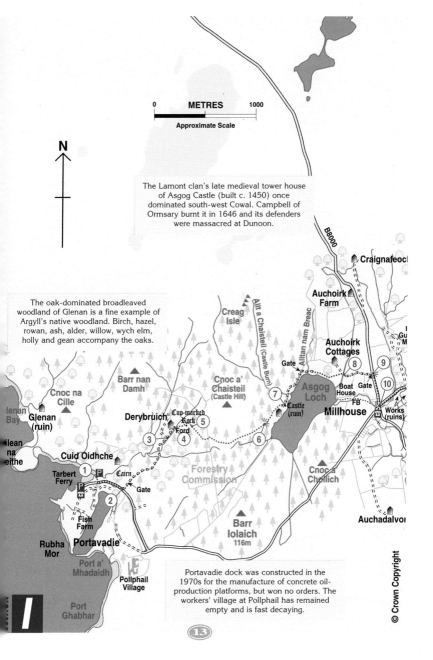

0   METRES   1000
Approximate Scale

N

The Lamont clan's late medieval tower house of Asgog Castle (built c. 1450) once dominated south-west Cowal. Campbell of Ormsary burnt it in 1646 and its defenders were massacred at Dunoon.

The oak-dominated broadleaved woodland of Glenan is a fine example of Argyll's native woodland. Birch, hazel, rowan, ash, alder, willow, wych elm, holly and gean accompany the oaks.

Portavadie dock was constructed in the 1970s for the manufacture of concrete oil-production platforms, but won no orders. The workers' village at Pollphail has remained empty and is fast decaying.

Craignafeoch

Auchoirk Farm

Auchoirk Cottages

Creag Isle

Cnoc a' Chaisteil (Castle Hill)

Barr nan Damh

Cnoc na Cille

Glenan (ruin)

lenan Bay

lean na eithe

Derybruich

Cup-marked Rock

Ford

Cuid Oidhche

Tarbert Ferry

Cairn

Gate

Fish Farm

Rubha Mor

Portavadie

Port a' Mhadaidh

Pollphail Village

Port Ghabhar

Forestry Commission

Barr Iolaich
116m

Cnoc a' Choilich

Auchadalvor

Asgog Loch

Boat House

Millhouse

Works (ruins)

Castle (ruin)

Gate

Allt a' Chaisteil (Castle Burn)

Alltan nam Breac

B8000

1
2
3
4
5
6
7
8
9
10

I

Turn L and follow it to the N corner of the loch (gate). 50m beyond the gate its line becomes very indistinct. Continue parallel to the shore to enter the next field below a broken, wooded 'hedge' running down from Auchoirk cottages. Walk uphill & R (150m) to a gatepost on the skyline (far side of the field & to R of cottages).

The Gunpowder Works Bell

■ **8** Follow the track (now obvious again) down to the B8000 road.

■ **9** Turn R on the B8000 to the Millhouse crossroads (300m).

■ **10** Turn L here on the road leading to Kames and Tighnabruaich. Follow it to a L bend opposite Cladh a Mhuilinn Lodge and a bell post (500m).

■ **11** Enter a field via a stile immediately L of the Lodge (Scottish Rights of Way Soc. sign). Cross this field (uphill, fence to R; 250m). Enter the next field by gate or stile to continue the same line. Narrow muddy paths allow you to rise between thick whin (gorse) for

c. 300m until you emerge into open ground. Ahead is impenetrable whin. To avoid it, cut L across the corner of the field for 100m or so (no path) towards a small gate in the L-running fence.

■ **12** Through the gate, go directly across to the nearby edge of a golf fairway (care!). Walk R, uphill, along the fairway's edge towards the green. At the near edge of the green, follow a ditch L across the fairway. At the far side begins a track which leads you to the L end of a conifer wood (250m in all).

■ **13** By the trees, a track comes in from the L. Ignore it. Follow the main track from the fairway to a second track in 400m. Turn R here, swing L, then R again to pass under electricity cables (200m). On your L, 60m beyond the cables, is a low grassy platform behind which a path descends L at a low-set sign ('to the shore').

■ **14** Follow the path, through woods, to the shore (1km). Car P.

■ **15** Turn L into Kames. Ignore all L turns along the way until forced to rise where the road zig-zags behind the Kames Hotel.

■ **16** Follow around the back of the hotel and continue (sea to your R) past the public toilets (R), uphill again past a newsagent / general store (L) to a crossroads on the B8000 (shops and PO).

■ **17** Turn R along the B8000 for Tighnabruaich. Regain the shore, pass a ruined pier & the A8003 junction (ignore) to (1.7km)....

■ **18** ....Tighnabruaich centre (GR 979728; shops/ PO). Several B&Bs & hotels here and in Kames.

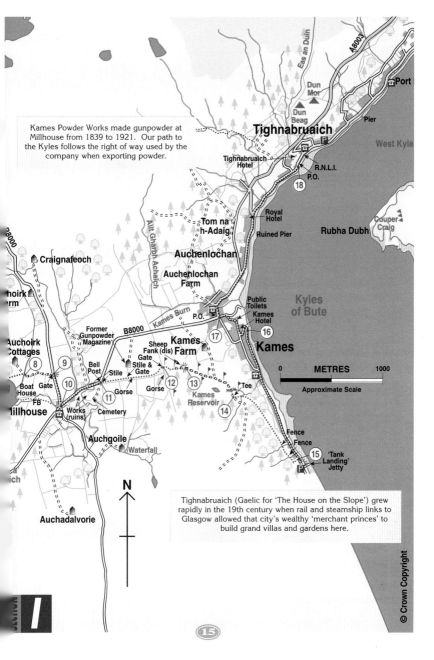

Kames Powder Works made gunpowder at Millhouse from 1839 to 1921. Our path to the Kyles follows the right of way used by the company when exporting powder.

Tighnabruaich (Gaelic for 'The House on the Slope') grew rapidly in the 19th century when rail and steamship links to Glasgow allowed that city's wealthy 'merchant princes' to build grand villas and gardens here.

N

METRES

Approximate Scale

© Crown Copyright

1

TIGHNABRUAICH - CLACHAN OF GLENDARUEL
13.9km (8.7 miles)

Route Details

Distance	13.9km (8.7 miles)
Degree of Difficulty	Moderate to Strenuous
Ascent	170m (560ft)
Time	5.5 hours

Start and Finish Points

Start: Tighnabruaich; shops, hotel and post office at GR 979728. Stagecoach Western & Wee Geoff's Buses run from Dunoon to T'bruaich most days. A Post Bus runs Dunoon - T'bruaich 2x daily (not Sun). Tel. post bus helpline 01246 546329. Taxis & Buses*
Finish: Clachan of Glendaruel at GR 996842 (Glendaruel Hotel). Buses: Wee Geoff's Buses, (schooldays only here). Taxis & Buses* (below)
*To contact Buses or local Taxis, see Section 1.

Maps Needed

OS Pathfinder Nos. 400 (NR 87/97); 401 (NS 07/17); 389 (NS 08/18) & 388 (NR 88/98). OS Landranger Nos. 62; 63 & 55.

Parking Facilities

Tighnabruaich at GR 983731. Glendaruel; near the hotel.

Route Description

■ **1** With your back to the post office, turn R; follow the shore road (sea to R) until, in 1.6km, the houses and tarmac end and a track continues by the shore.
■ **2** Cross a boatyard slipway. Ahead, 350m away, your track can be seen rising below a grey crag. Follow the track past the crag to Rubha Ban headland.
■ **3** Follow the track by the shore for a further 600m to a fork.
■ **4** At the fork, take the L track, which rises into woods. Go uphill for 300m to a R bend by a concrete bridge & waterfall. After 100m more the track levels out for 50m, and rounds a L bend to reach a junction (deer fence to L).
■ **5** Continue straight ahead (descending) to regain the shore in 400m. A further 400m brings an open view across a small S-facing bay to a rocky headland and a disused white lighthouse.
■ **6** Continue N along the track for 150m to the head of the small bay. After 120m more, with a second bay to the R, the track bends L then (50m) sharp R (ignore L branch here) to reach a 'crossways' in another 100m.
■ **7** At the 'crossways', ignore the L branch (seven steps) and the R (track to three houses). Continue ahead with the main track into thick wood and rhododendron. The track soon curves R and rises to a level summit before returning to sea-level (400m). Continue 400m more to a cattle grid, then into open country, to arrive (150m) between two metal

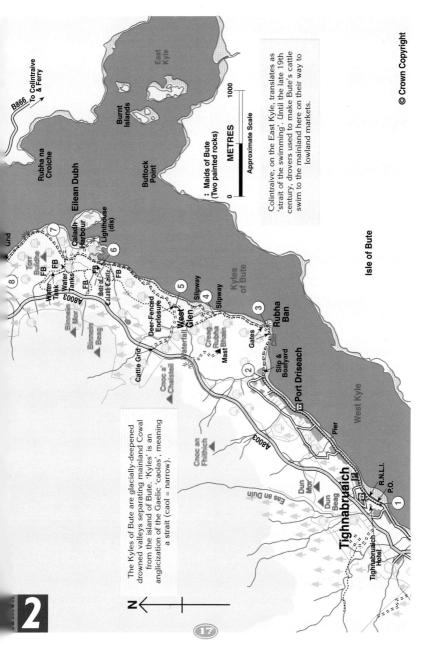

N ←

2

17

© Crown Copyright

B866
To Colintraive & Ferry

Grid

To Colintraive & Ferry

East Kyle

Burnt Islands

Rubha na Croiche

Eilean Dubh

Caladh Harbour

Lighthouse (dis)

Buttock Point

∴ Maids of Bute (Two painted rocks)

METRES
0   1000
Approximate Scale

Colintraive, on the East Kyle, translates as 'strait of the swimming'. Until the late 19th century, drovers used to make Bute's cattle swim to the mainland here on their way to lowland markets.

Isle of Bute

Torr Buidhe

FB

Water Tank

Water Tanks

FB

FB

Caladh Castle

Sgeir of Caladh Castle

FB

A8003

Binnein Mor

Binnein Beag

Cattle Grid

Croc a' Chaisteil

Deer-Fenced Enclosure

West Glen

Waterfall

Slipway

Slipway

Mast Bhein

Creag Rubha Bhain

Gates

Kyles of Bute

Rubha Ban

Cliff

Slip & Boatyard

Port Driseach

Gates

Croc an Fhithich

A8003

Pier

Dun Mor

Eas an Duin

Dun Beag

Dun Dun

West Kyle

Tighnabruaich

Tighnabruaich Hotel

R.N.L.I.

P.O.

The Kyles of Bute are glacially-deepened drowned valleys separating mainland Cowal from the island of Bute. Kyles is an anglicization of the Gaelic 'caolas', meaning a strait (caol = narrow).

sheds. Beyond the sheds are two white houses. Before they are reached, a sign, ('Footpath to Ormidale') indicates your path leading R to the shore.

Tighnabruaich and the Kyles of Bute

■ **8** CARE: the next 1.4km to Craig Lodge are a much tougher 'walk within a walk'. In dry weather, with the tide less than high and before bracken grows tall, it's still rough, but if these conditions are reversed it is a longer job and could occupy upwards of an hour. Anyone with a heavy pack will need to balance carefully.

Go down the path to the stony beach. Turn L and follow it N below houses and four small fields, crossing three small burns, before steep ground comes close to the shore again immediately beyond the fence corner at the north end of the last field (400m). If the tide is high, you can get along between Points 8 and 9 on grass above the shore. The first few tens of metres (near the houses) may be the most awkward.

■ **9a** If possible, continue along the shore for about 500m to reach a group of massive fallen boulders, some on the upper shore, and some on the land just above. Some are

several metres high. There are fish cages offshore, and a boatshed and slip across the loch.

■ **9b** IF the tide is high enough to block progress beyond the field end / fence corner, you must take a narrow, but well-trodden, path that generally takes a raised beach level a handful of metres above the shore. It rises and falls, through thickets of trees, rhododendron and bracken but is continuous where needed, and is only rarely faint. There are one or two markers on this section (small yellow arrows) but they are easily missed. At high tide your first obstacle is 20m past the fence corner - a set of gently-sloping but slippery rock slabs bars the way. Climb on to these a metre or so (steep step) just where they begin, passing over some small moss-covered boulders behind a whin (gorse) bush to an isolated 1m high boulder on top of the slabs. A couple of metres further is a second boulder on the grass behind the slabs - beside it (about 30m from the fence) the narrow trodden path appears. Follow it closely as it twists and turns, rises and falls, never more than a few metres above the sea. Care is required in some narrow, steep places. After 500m (the second half close beside the shore again) reach the large boulders mentioned above (9 (a)).

■ **10** Pass beyond the largest boulders, or squeeze between them where they lean together. By medium-sized boulders (2m or so) immediately beyond the largest ones, two pieces of black and white tape are tied to rhododendrons. The

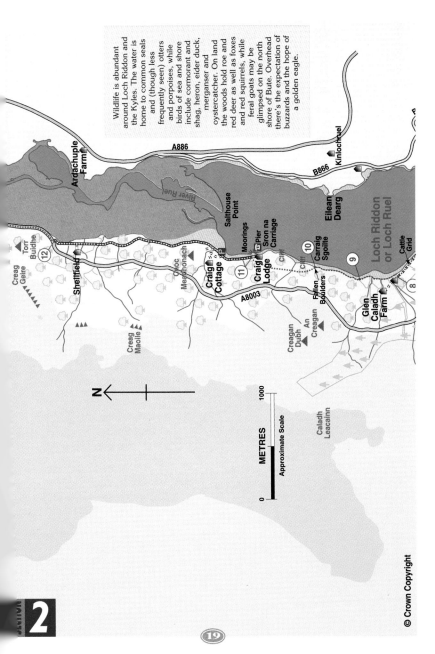

Wildlife is abundant around Loch Riddon and the Kyles. The water is home to common seals and (though less frequently seen) otters and porpoises, while birds of sea and shore include cormorant and shag, heron, eider duck, merganser and oystercatcher. On land the woods hold roe and red deer as well as foxes and red squirrels, while feral goats may be glimpsed on the north shore of Bute. Overhead there's the expectation of buzzards and the hope of a golden eagle.

Ardachuple Farm

A886

River Ruel

Salthouse Point

Kinlochruel

B866

Eilean Dearg

Loch Riddon or Loch Ruel

Moorings

Pier
Sron na
Carriage

Cliff

Craig
Cottage

Craig
Lodge

(11)

Cnoc
Meadhonach

Carraig
Sgoilte

(10)

Cliff

(9)

Cattle
Grid

Sheilfield

Torr
Buidhe

(12)

Creag
Geire

Creag
Maoile

A8003

Fallen
Boulders

Glen
Caladh
Farm

(8)

Creagan
Dubh

An
Creagan

N

METRES

0   1000

Approximate Scale

Caladh
Leacainn

narrow, trodden path rises between the tapes into the woods. Take great care to find it, as any other way would be a fight.

Similar marker tapes, as well as several 10cm square signs (bold yellow arrows on a green ground nailed to branches or trunks at roughly head height) are found between here and Craig Lodge, but you will still need to follow the trodden line carefully.

Once on the path, follow it to Craig Lodge (500m, slow going) often through thick bracken and / or rhododendron as well as trees, rising eventually to 50m or more above the sea. At one point, cross a burn awkwardly (steep step down, steeper up) at a point just below a 4m high crag which rises above the far bank. Occasionally the line of the path needs to be looked for with care. On descent, when the roof of Craig Lodge becomes visible steeply below you, the path splits and rejoins variously, crossing more open ground. Take CARE as to your balance here, especially if carrying a heavy load. Emerge on to the public road beyond the house immediately past its gates.

■ **11** Turn L onto the tarmac road at Craig Lodge and follow it N for 2km to its junction with the A8003 main Tighnabruaich road.

■ **12** Turn R (Dunoon direction) onto the main road. The route is obvious throughout, but take care as much of it is single track and it's often busy. Unfortunately there is no good alternative to following this road N for the next flat 3.4km to a point, just before it crosses the River

Ruel, where there is a L turn (GR 999826: house on L & signs 'Waulkmill' & 'B&B').

Port Driseach from Tighnabruaich Pier

■ **13** Follow the side road L from Waulkmill. It's disused for cars beyond the house and becoming mossy. Come in 600m to a bridge over the Bealachandrain Burn. Cross with care (passable only on foot as its L half has collapsed) to find yourself at a T-junction.

■ **14** Turn R: go 150m to cross the River Ruel by a two-arch Telford bridge of 1808 (see p.21). Once over the bridge, turn L to follow the line of the road gently uphill for 350m to its junction with the A886.

■ **15** Turn L here on to the A886, in the direction signposted 'Glasgow'. Follow this road N for 300m, as far as the L turning signposted 'Clachan of Glendaruel' (CARE: it's not an especially busy main road, but is double track and very fast. Use grass verges if necessary).

■ **16** Turn L and follow the side road for 350m into Clachan of Glendaruel, where to-day's section ends....

■ **17**....in front of the Glendaruel Hotel.

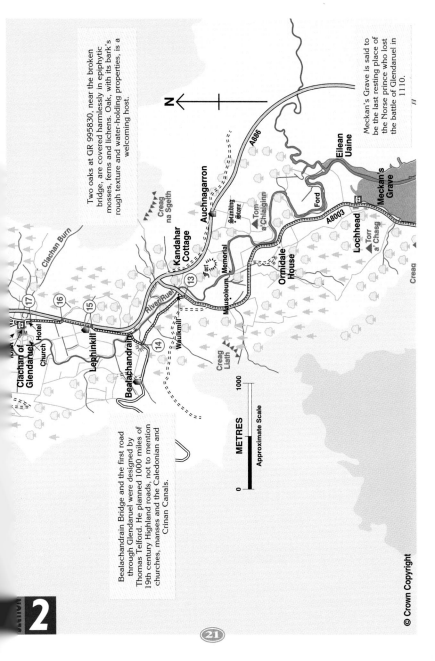

N ←

Two oaks at GR 995830, near the broken bridge, are covered harmlessly in epiphytic mosses, ferns and lichens. Oak, with its bark's rough texture and water-holding properties, is a welcoming host.

Meckan's Grave is said to be the last resting place of the Norse prince who lost the battle of Glendaruel in 1110.

Bealachandrain Bridge and the first road through Glendaruel were designed by Thomas Telford. He planned 1000 miles of 19th century Highland roads, not to mention churches, manses and the Caledonian and Crinan Canals.

METRES

0   1000

Approximate Scale

Clachan Burn

Creag na Sgeith

A886

Auchnagarron

Kandahar Cottage

Standing Stone

Tom a'Chlaiginn

Eilean Uaine

Meckan's Grave

Clachan of Glendaruel

Church   Hotel

17

16

15

Lephinkill

River Ruel

13

Fort

Mausoleum Memorial

Ormidale House

Ford

A8003

Lochhead

Torr a' Chasg

Creag

Bealachandrain

14

Waulkmill

Creag Liath

© Crown Copyright

2

SECTION **3**

GLENDARUEL
9.1km (5.7 miles)

Route Details

Distance	9.1km (5.7 miles)
Degree of Difficulty	Very Easy
Ascent	60m (200ft)
Time	3.5 hours

Start and Finish Points

Start: Clachan of Glendaruel
(Glendaruel Hotel; GR 996842)
Buses: Wee Geoff's Buses, 01700
811473 (schooldays, infrequent).
Taxis: see Section 1
Finish: GR 037910: Junction of
A886 with West Glendaruel Road.
Accommodation here is limited;
see notes under point 12, or
arrange transport back to
Clachan of Glendaruel or further
south. Buses and taxis as above.

Maps Needed

OS Pathfinder No. 388 (NR
88/98); No. 389 (NS 08/18); No.
379 (NS 09/19) OS Landranger
No. 55

Parking Facilities

Glendaruel: adequate near hotel.
Very limited at N end of
the walk.

Route Description

Follow the very quiet West
Glendaruel Road throughout.
■ **1** With your back to Glendaruel
Hotel's front door, turn L and walk
N past the phone box (ignore L turn
to church). After less than 100m,
fork L (narrow). In 60m more, rejoin
a branch of the wider road and
descend to a stone bridge over the
River Ruel.
■ **2** Cross the bridge, and follow the
road for 500m across the flat flood
plain to the foot of the western hill
slopes, where it stays all through
the glen. Camquhart Farm is
reached in another 450m.
■ **3** The scale of the Camquhart
Farm buildings reflects the unusual
richness (for Argyll) of this lower
part of Glendaruel; arable crops
such as barley can be grown.
Round the first L bend beyond the
farm, a small line of roadside crags
represents an old sea cliff from a
time when the late ice age sea
flooded the glen. Continue for
another 1km along the road, past
Maymore Farm, to a track
signposted (R) for the main road
(ignore). In the fork between road
and track is an abandoned gothic
gateway.
■ **4** Continue L of this (the
'Lucknow Gate') passing Home
Farm (holiday homes) and, in
600m, a disused walled garden
once belonging to Glendaruel
House. Hidden behind Home Farm,
the 'big house' site is now
Glendaruel caravan and campsite.
■ **5** Beyond the walled garden, the
road curves R, then runs straight for

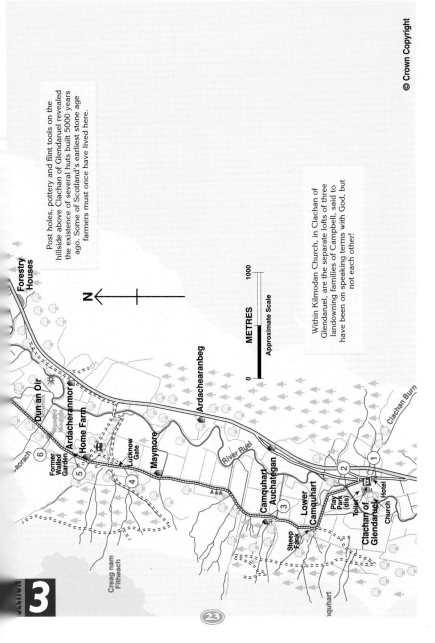

Post holes, pottery and flint tools on the hillside above Clachan of Glendaruel revealed the existence of several huts built 5000 years ago. Some of Scotland's earliest stone age farmers must once have lived here.

Within Kilmodan Church, in Clachan of Glendaruel, are the separate lofts of three landowning families of Campbell, said to have been on speaking terms with God, but not each other!

© Crown Copyright

N

METRES

Approximate Scale

0   1000

Forestry Houses

Dun an Oir

Ardacheranmor

Former Walled Garden

Home Farm

Lucknow Gate

Maymore

Ardachearanbeg

Camquhart Auchategan

Lower Camquhart

River Ruel

Play Park (dis)

Toilet

Clachan of Glendaruel

Church Hotel

Sheep Fank

Creag nam Fitheach

Clachan Burn

nearly 1km, climbing a little. Walk about 150m along this straight.
■ **6** Here, at GR 001873, four elongated wooded mounds can be seen (R) on the glen floor (between GR 002872 and GR 004875). They represent meltwater deposits from beneath the Glendaruel Glacier. The nearby hillock of Dun an Oir holds the burial ground of the Campbells of Glendaruel. Continue along the road past the house of Clacheranmor (L, 400m beyond Dun an Oir).
■ **7** Just past the house, in the field on the R, rises a mound, partly screened by scrub and trees - a medieval 'motte', or fortified hill. Between this point and Achanelid Farm, notice the many-stemmed hazels on the R, perhaps the effect of long-ago coppicing?
■ **8** Between Achanelid and the cattle grid at GR 018886 (1.6km), the road drops back to flood plain level. It is now a very different glen, rush-infested, with poor drainage.
■ **9** Just beyond the cattle grid at GR 018886 a faint, rough track rises steeply up the hill to the L. Though off our route, it leads to the ruined farming township of Kildalvan on a glen-side terrace at about 110m (GR 017889). Continue NE along the road for about 600m to a barn on the L.
■ **10** Another 800m takes you to a long passing place on a slight rise, giving good views to the white farmhouse of Strondavon which overlooks the start of Section 4. Farther off, and high up, may appear the ragged outline of Creag Tharsuinn beyond the Garvie Glen.

Continue along the road for 600m to a stone barn with traditional long ventilation slits (GR 029903).

Kilmodan Church, Glendaruel

■ **11** From 100m beyond the barn, at the top of a rise in the road, you can see across the glen floor, beyond Garvie Farm, into the Garvie Glen - the route of Section 4. Don't be tempted to cut straight across - instead continue along the west glen road, past the L fork to Kilbridemore Farm (ignore), to reach the bridge over the Kilbridemore Burn in another 300m and....
■ **12** ....the junction with the A886 road in a further 500m (end of Section 3). Accommodation here is limited. Try Glendaruel caravan & campsite (01369 820267; see point 4) or Achanelid Farm (01369 820225; point 8) or Old Kilmodan School (01369 820377; GR 025889). Ask locally, but it may be necessary to find transport elsewhere (also limited) or to continue - at least to Glenbranter, if not to Strachur.

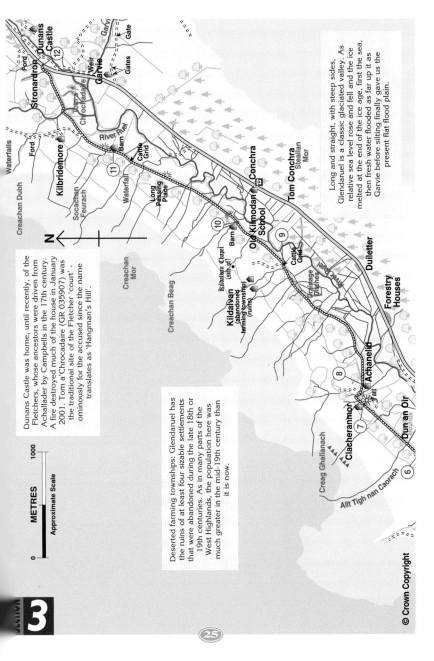

Dunans Castle was home, until recently, of the Fletchers, whose ancestors were driven from Achallader by Campbells in the 17th century. A fire destroyed much of the house in January 2001. Tom a'Chrocadaire (GR 035907) was the traditional site of the Fletcher 'court' - ominously for the accused since the name translates as 'Hangman's Hill'.

Deserted farming townships: Glendaruel has the ruins of at least four sizable settlements that were abandoned during the late 18th or 19th centuries. As in many parts of the West Highlands, the population here was much greater in the mid-19th century than it is now.

Long and straight, with steep sides, Glendaruel is a classic glaciated valley. As relative sea level rose and fell and the ice melted at the end of the ice age, first the sea, then fresh water flooded as far up it as Garvie before silting finally gave us the present flat flood plain.

METRES
0   1000
Approximate Scale

N

Waterfalls

Creachan Dubh

Stronardrox

Dunans Castle (12)

Garvie

Garvie

Gate

Ford

Weir

Gates

Kilbridemore

River Ruel

Barn

(11)

Cattle Grid

Socachan Feurach

Waterfall

Long Passing Place

Creachan Mor

Creachan Beag

Kilbalkin Chapel (site of)

Kildalvan (abandoned farming township) (ruins)

Barn

(10)

Old Kilmodan School

Conchra

Tom Conchra

Steallan Mor

Cattle Grid

(9)

Drainage Ditches

Ruel River

Duiletter

Forestry Houses

Creag Ghallanach

Clacheranmor

(7)

(8)

Achanelid

Fort

Dun an Oir

Allt Tigh nan Caorach

(6)

© Crown Copyright

GLENDARUEL - GLENBRANTER
14.5km (9.1 miles)

Route Details

Distance	14.5km (9.1 miles)
Degree of Difficulty	Easy
Ascent	380m (1250ft)
Time	5.5 hours

Start and Finish Points

Start: Junction of the West Glendaruel Road with the A886 at GR 037910. Buses & Taxis: see Section 3. Finish: Road junction at GR 113980, 100m NE of Glenbranter forest village.
Buses: Stagecoach Western Buses (01369 707701) run (not Sun.) between Dunoon and Strachur, Inveraray & (less frequently) Lochgoilhead and Carrick Castle, stopping on the nearby A815.
Taxis: nearest are in Dunoon (26km / 16 miles).

Maps Needed

OS Pathfinder No. 389 (NS 08/18) (for less than 1km); No. 379 (NN 09/19); OS Landranger No. 56

Parking Facilities

At the start - very limited.
At Glenbranter: GR 111977

Route Description

■ **1** From the road junction at GR 037910, walk S, downhill, along the verge of the A886. Cross two bridges, ignoring track junctions (L) before and after, before rising to a track junction on the L immediately beyond the house of Garvie Farm (750m; sign). CARE: the road, if not busy, is fast.

■ **2** Turn L onto the track leading behind the farmhouse and go up towards the farm steading (broadleaved trees to R and Garvie farm buildings to your L). Passing through the top of the farmyard (2 gates in quick succession) the track emerges, 200m from the main road, into rough open pastureland with lots of rushes. (The top corner of the farmyard can be by-passed to its right if stock are being worked within it).

■ **3** Follow the (obvious) track steadily uphill across the rough field, passing through another gate at 300m from the farm. About 150m beyond this gate the track enters the first of several stretches of scrubby broadleaves - birch, hazel, willow etc. - and in a further 100m or so begins to climb steeply, turning a short succession of sharp bends, above which it again becomes gentler. Pass beneath electricity cables and, 200m further on, find another track coming in from the R at a sharp angle.

■ **4** Ignore the track from the R and carry straight on. Pass L of a conifer plantation, descending steeply to a concrete bridge over the Leth Allt. Ignore a short track (L) to a

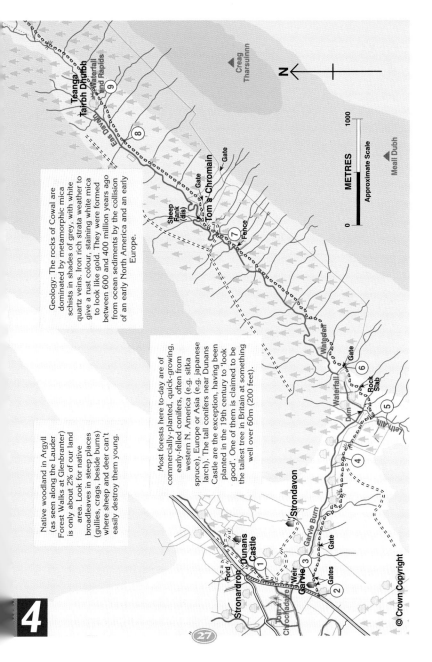

Geology: The rocks of Cowal are dominated by metamorphic mica schists in shades of grey, with white quartz veins. Iron rich strata weather to give a rust colour, staining white mica to look like gold. They were formed between 600 and 400 million years ago from ocean sediments by the collision of an early North America and an early Europe.

Native woodland in Argyll (as seen along the Lauder Forest Walks at Glenbranter) is only about 2% of our land area. Look for native broadleaves in steep places (gullies, crags, beside burns) where sheep and deer can't easily destroy them young.

Most forests here to-day are of commercially-planted, quick-growing, early-felled conifers, often from western N. America (e.g. sitka spruce), Europe or Asia (e.g. japanese larch). The tall conifers near Dunans Castle are the exception, having been planted in the 19th century to 'look good'. One of them is claimed to be the tallest tree in Britain at something well over 60m (200 feet).

Creag Tharsuinn

Meall Dubh

N

METRES

Approximate Scale

0   1000

Teanga Tarbh Dhubh

Waterfall and Rapids ⑨

⑧

Eas Daraich

Gate

Gate

Sheep Fank (dis)

Tom a'Chromain

Fence ⑦

Waterfall

Wategean

Gate ⑥

Rock Slab

Dam

Leth-Allt

⑤

④

Garvie Burn

Strondavon

Stronardron Dunans Castle

Ford

① Garvie Weir

Gate

② Gates

③

Dun a' Chocladaire

© Crown Copyright

4

27

corrugated iron shack above the hidden dam on the Garvie Burn.

■ **5** Cross the Leth Allt by the concrete bridge, and follow the track as it rises steeply L (ignore another short branch that descends L). At 300m from the bridge, in a burn to your right, a slab of the local schist rock dips down to the NW, a tiny part of the NW 'limb' of the 'Cowal Arch' (see page 29). Another 200m brings you to a gate leading into the forest.

■ **6** Pass through the gate, and continue on the track, which now runs very gently uphill, keeping to the R (SE) side of the Eas Davain burn. After a little over 100m, a waterfall (about 6 or 7m in total height) is glimpsed below on the main burn. Continue easily along the track, through conifer plantations of various ages, for nearly 2km. This brings you to the next track junction.

■ **7** Here a track goes off to the L at 90°, to cross the river straight away by a concrete bridge. Across this bridge there has been much felling in recent years and signs of windthrow are evident L and high up. Do not cross the bridge, but continue straight ahead on the previous line. A short turning loop goes off to the R - ignore. After 150m, the track curves R (old stone sheep fank soon on L) then bends back L; a gate used by all-terrain vehicles leads up (R) through open ground, but ignore it and continue on the track for a further 1km (making 3 gently-sloping km in all). Notice a fenced enclosure on the opposite bank after about 800m.

■ **8** Beyond a R bend, the track rises again more steeply. After about 500m of this ascent, a small branch of track on the L (a turning area) marks a good point to view a small series of cascades above you on the Eas Davain.

Looking back to Garvie Farm

■ **9** From the turning place by the falls, continue to follow the track uphill to the NE. After about 400m it becomes much gentler and from this flatter section a view forward opens up through a boggy clearing along the line of an old fence. In the distance can be seen Beinn Bhuidhe, an isolated 'Munro' well over 25km away. Continue, rising again, for another 600m to a point where a 15m wide never-planted gap opens in the forest to the right, above a black peat bank. This gap, which widens rapidly uphill, has a ruined fence on its R margin. The highest stretch of to-day's walk begins less than 200m ahead at the next unplanted gap on the R of the track.

■ **10** The track's summit 'level' runs from here for 300m, where another unplanted gap through the trees appears on the R.

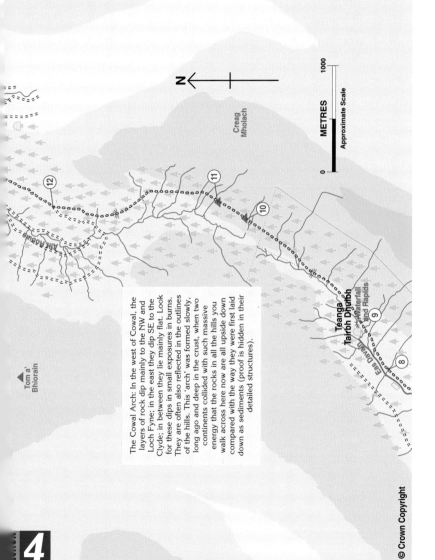

The Cowal Arch: In the west of Cowal, the layers of rock dip mainly to the NW and Loch Fyne; in the east they dip SE to the Clyde; in between they lie mainly flat. Look for these dips in small exposures in burns. They are often also reflected in the outlines of the hills. This 'arch' was formed slowly, long ago and deep in the crust, when two continents collided with such massive energy that the rocks in all the hills you walk across here now are all upside down compared with the way they were first laid down as sediments (proof is hidden in their detailed structures).

Tom a' Bhiorain

Creag Mholach

N

METRES
0   1000
Approximate Scale

Allt Robuic

Teanga Tairbh Dhuibh
Waterfall and Rapids

Eas Dubh

4

29

© Crown Copyright

11 This gap marks the end of the highest part. Continue downhill (gently at first, steeper later) into upper Glen Branter. After a further 600m, a track joins from the L.

12 Ignore the track from the L but carry on down R. As you descend, many clear-felled areas of forest reveal new views out across lower Glen Branter and the strath of the River Cur to the mountains opposite, notably Beinn Bheula (a 'Corbett' at over 2500ft). Go round a sharp L bend followed by a long turn to the R, still descending; Beinn Mhor lies ahead as you face S. A green track comes in from the L.

13 Ignore this grassy and mossy L turn. Instead carry straight on (red cycle marker) for another 150m or so to a point where our stony, well-used track swings sharply L and sets off steeply downhill. Ignore a straight ahead option and instead turn L with the main track

The Beinn Bheula group from Glenbranter

14 At the beginning of the steep descent is another red cycle marker. Continue down for 500m to where the track flattens out to cross a big burn by a large culvert. Near the foot of the hill, ignore a path on

the L (Lauder Forest Walks) and a much less-used track from the R.

15 Beyond the culvert-bridge, where the track swings R, there are very mature conifers to your R. To the L is (first) another branch of the Lauder paths and then a large turning circle. Ignore these, continuing on and down to walk near the L bank of a large, stony burn. The track then briefly rises to a gate, beyond which are houses. Pass them to their R and descend to a junction just beyond the point where our track becomes a metalled road.

16 Ignore the track to the L, but continue on the metalled road beside the L bank of the burn, passing the bridge to Glenshellish Farm after another 150m.

17 Continue on the tarmac L of the burn. Another 250m brings you to a muddy track on the R (ignore). The road leaves the burn here and goes straight for 200m; ahead is the 1950s forestry village of Glenbranter. Do not go through the small group of wooden houses, but instead turn 90° L and follow the road uphill, then round to the R, to by-pass the village on its L. Ignore tracks on the L, which lead to the Lauder walks car park, but instead follow the curve of the road round past the village to reach....

18 ....the road junction at GR 113980 through a pair of sandstone pillars. This is the end of Section 4. Ask about accommodation locally, but you might need to go on to Strachur (5km: a few B&Bs & 1 hotel) or towards Dunoon (hotels at 6 and 11km in that direction).

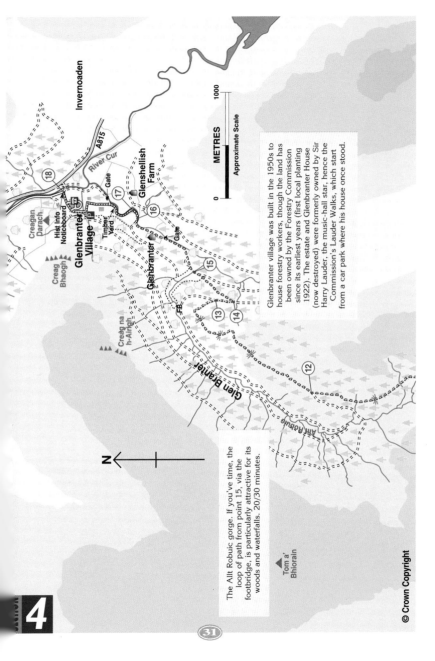

N ←

Invernoaden

A815

River Cur

Creagan Darach

Hist Info Noticeboard

Glenbranter Village

Creag Bhaogh

Creag na h-Airigh

Gate

(18)

Glenshellish Farm

(17)

(16)

Timber Yard

Glenbranter

Gate

(15)

(13)

(14)

FB

Glen Branter

Allt Robuic

(12)

Tom a' Bhiorain

Glenbranter village was built in the 1950s to house forestry workers, though the land has been owned by the Forestry Commission since its earliest years (first local planting 1922). The estate and Glenbranter House (now destroyed) were formerly owned by Sir Harry Lauder, the music-hall star, hence the Commission's Lauder Walks, which start from a car park where his house once stood.

The Allt Robuic gorge. If you've time, the loop of path from point 15, via the footbridge, is particularly attractive for its woods and waterfalls. 20/30 minutes.

METRES

0   1000

Approximate Scale

(31)

© Crown Copyright

GLENBRANTER - LOCHGOILHEAD
17.6km (11 miles)

Route Details

Distance	17.6km (11 miles)
Degree of Difficulty	Strenuous
Ascent	210m (689ft)
Time	7 hours

Start and Finish Points

Start: Road junction at GR 113980, 100m NE of Glenbranter forest village, W of river bridge. Buses & Taxis: see Section 4.
Finish: Lochgoilhead PO at GR 200012. Buses to Strachur and Dunoon (M to F, schooldays; M & F only, other times; Stagecoach Western Buses, 01369 707701) & also to Helensburgh via Ardgartan, Arrochar, Tarbet, Inverbeg & Luss. (M to Sat; Garelochhead Minibuses, 01436 810200)

Maps Needed

OS Pathfinder No. 379 (NS 09/19); No. 367 (NN 00/10); No. 368 (NN 20/30) (for a tiny distance)
OS Landranger No. 56

Parking Facilities

Glenbranter: at GR 111977 (Lauder Forest Walks) Lochgoilhead: at GR 199012 (PO)

Route Description

■ **1** From the sandstone pillars at GR 113980, with your back to Glenbranter village, turn L immediately onto the former main road. Follow this quiet road all the way to its junction with the main A815 at the outskirts of Strachur village (4km).
■ **2** Cross the A815 (with care, fast bend) and take the side road nearly opposite (slightly R). Ignore an early L turn, but go down and up again, to turn sharp R, after another 250m, behind a long conifer wood. In another 400m turn L at a junction (sign 'Succoth Farm').
■ **3** Follow the road uphill for 500m to a cattle grid.
■ **4** Descend beyond the cattle grid to enter (mainly) broadleaved woodland after about 150m. Approx. 1km from the cattle grid is a forest track to L - ignore. The road descends to cross the River Cur by a bridge (another 150m).
■ **5** Go straight on (20m) to cross a second (timber) bridge over the Leavanin Burn. CARE: three holes, no parapet and it's slippery when wet. Once across the bridge, our route (a mossy track) enters the forest (gate and stile). Go steeply uphill for 1km, ignoring two tracks that enter from the R at 150 and 500m. The angle eases for the last 100m or so before the track forks.
■ **6** The L fork descends; ignore it and continue gently uphill, slightly R, for nearly 1km to reach a junction with a very stony track.
■ **7** Turn L and follow this track for 100m, up a short rise. At its top is

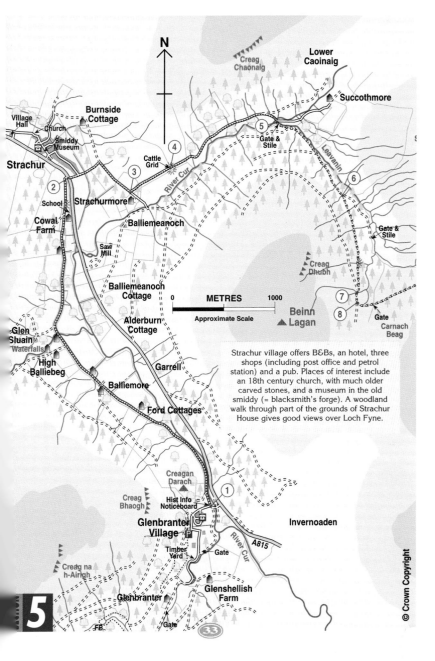

N

Lower
Caoinaig

Creag
Chaonaig

Succothmore

Burnside
Cottage

Village
Hall

Church

Smiddy
Museum

Strachur

Cattle
Grid

④

⑤

Gate &
Stile

River Cur

Leanamin

⑥

②

School

Strachurmore

③

Cowal
Farm

Balliemeanoch

Gate &
Stile

Saw
Mill

Creag
Dhubh

⑦

Balliemeanoch
Cottage

⑧

Gate

0   METRES   1000

Beinn
Lagan

Carnach
Beag

Alderburn
Cottage

Approximate Scale

Glen
Sluain

Waterfalls

Strachur village offers B&Bs, an hotel, three
shops (including post office and petrol
station) and a pub. Places of interest include
an 18th century church, with much older
carved stones, and a museum in the old
smiddy (= blacksmith's forge). A woodland
walk through part of the grounds of Strachur
House gives good views over Loch Fyne.

High
Balliebeg

Garrell

Balliemore

Ford Cottages

Creagan
Darach

Creag
Bhaogh

Hist Info
Noticeboard

①

Invernoaden

Glenbranter
Village

River Cur

A815

Creag na
h-Airigh

Timber
Yard

Gate

Glenbranter

Glenshellish
Farm

FB

Gate

33

5

© Crown Copyright

another track junction.
■ **8** Turn L on this new track. It bends R, then L, to re-enter the forest at a gate 200m away. Follow it E, rising gently for another 1.1km, to its end. From here a narrower, well-surfaced 'all-terrain vehicle' (ATV) track continues 100m more, to emerge from the forest at a fence and gate.

Curra Lochain from the west

■ **9** Follow the ATV track out of the forest to its end c. 150m beyond the gate.
■ **10** From the path end, head approx. N across tussocks (no path, slow) to the main Leavanin Burn about 50m away in an open grassy gully. Turn R along the gully, passing a long 'waterslide' (don't cross - slippery; it's easier at a flat section about 50m above the waterslide - c.100m from the end of the ATV path).
■ **11** Cross the burn and head straight up (N) towards the trees. Look carefully for the faded tyre tracks of an ATV close to and parallel with the forest edge. Turn

right (E) to follow these tracks for 300m up towards the Bealach an Lochain. Just before a point where the forest ahead comes much closer to the Leavanin Burn, turn into a wide ride that leads up L for 100m through the trees to the fence at the top of the forest. There's a stile in the fence to the R of the ride's top (GR 146002), above a short steeper slope.
■ **12** Cross the stile to open hill. Turn R to follow the forest fence (keep it on your R) all the way to the Curra Lochain. The going by the fence is often very wet, so it's best to stay well above it on steeper, but sometimes drier, ground. Look for sheep trods. At GR 149001 (300m from the stile) pass a sheep fank (pen) directly above the Bealach an Lochain pass (Curra Lochain now visible: Curra = Heron).
■ **13** Follow the fence as before till above the loch, then continue along its N shore (intermittent fishermen's path). Continue to the outflow at the loch's E end. (Care in last 80m where the way is more broken).
■ **14** CARE: The Curra Lochain outflow burn must be crossed. In spate it can be difficult.
If you don't mind wet feet, the gravelly bed at the burn's beginning gives good footing. There are stepping stones here, but they're unstable and often slippery. If you cross here, then follow the burn down on its opposite bank to where the fence crosses the burn at GR 162996. The best alternative crossing is a flat-topped 'island boulder' c. 170m downstream (c. 15m above the fence crossing). The

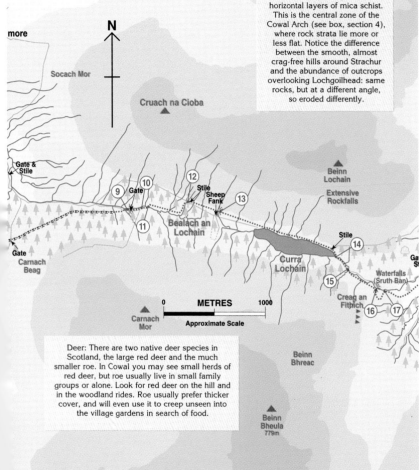

Sruth Ban waterfall tumbles over horizontal layers of mica schist. This is the central zone of the Cowal Arch (see box, section 4), where rock strata lie more or less flat. Notice the difference between the smooth, almost crag-free hills around Strachur and the abundance of outcrops overlooking Lochgoilhead: same rocks, but at a different angle, so eroded differently.

N

more

Socach Mor

Cruach na Cioba

Beinn Lochain

Gate & Stile

9 10 Gate 12 Stile 13 Sheep Fank

Extensive Rockfalls

11 Bealach an Lochain

Stile 14

Gate Carnach Beag

Curra Lochain

15 Stile Gate St

Waterfalls (Sruth Ban)

Creag an Fithich

16 17

0   METRES   1000

Carnach Mor

Approximate Scale

Deer: There are two native deer species in Scotland, the large red deer and the much smaller roe. In Cowal you may see small herds of red deer, but roe usually live in small family groups or alone. Look for red deer on the hill and in the woodland rides. Roe usually prefer thicker cover, and will even use it to creep unseen into the village gardens in search of food.

Beinn Bhreac

Beinn Bheula
779m

near bank giving access to the boulder is steep, but manageable with care. The step from the boulder to the S bank is easy.

■ **15** Having crossed the burn, and reached the fence crossing at GR 162996, continue down the glen on a very wet 'trod', passing a waterfall early on. After about 300m approach a big drop to a lower glen. Above it, the burn divides into two channels (GR 165994). This is the beginning of the sequence of falls known as Sruth Ban.

■ **16** Two small cliffs (2m and 4m), close together beside the 'path', mark the spot where it swings R away from the falls. It isn't possible to walk down close beside the falls all the way to their foot as a band of cliffs at half height bars the way. You must go more than 100m away from the stream before coming back below the biggest fall. Boggy trods mark a wet and tussocky line around the crags. If in doubt, work further away from the falls. Sruth Ban is not passable on the opposite (N) bank.

■ **17** Below the biggest fall is the last steep slope to the glen floor. Follow a rough trod down, but bear away R before the lowest point of the lowest fall to enter a gap in the forest (clearly seen from your terrace above). This gap runs about 100m or so R of the waterfall burn, until it brings you to the Lettermay Burn at GR 170995 (via an open gateway (& stile) in an old fence).

■ **18** Follow the Lettermay Burn downstream on its L bank, through a gap in the trees, to come out just above its confluence (GR 170996)

with the burn from Sruth Ban. CARE: You must cross the Lettermay here. In spate conditions, this burn can be difficult or even dangerous to cross. There is no easy alternative to a long retreat. It is often difficult to cross with dry feet. On the opposite bank, turn L and walk downstream, close to the bank (boggy in places), for about 800m. The glen steepens at a small brick building close to the water. A track leads R from here.

Sruth Ban Waterfalls

■ **19** Follow the track uphill (150m) to a junction. Turn L and follow it downhill for 1.3km to emerge from the forest at GR 187998.

■ **20** The track curves L (house) then R (houses) to join the public road at GR 188002 (500m).

■ **21** Turn L: follow the road for 2km around the head of Loch Goil and beside the River Goil to meet the B839 road at GR 198018.

■ **22** Turn R over a stone bridge. Follow the obvious main road for 600m to Lochgoilhead's centre ....

■ **23** .... at GR 200012: end of section 5. PO, shops & services.

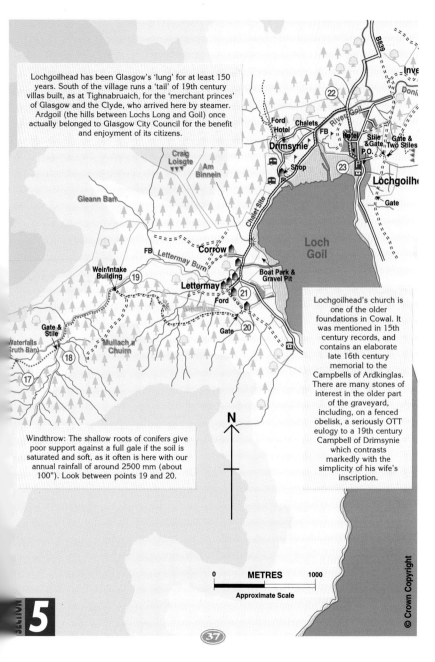

Lochgoilhead has been Glasgow's 'lung' for at least 150 years. South of the village runs a 'tail' of 19th century villas built, as at Tighnabruaich, for the 'merchant princes' of Glasgow and the Clyde, who arrived here by steamer. Ardgoil (the hills between Lochs Long and Goil) once actually belonged to Glasgow City Council for the benefit and enjoyment of its citizens.

Lochgoilhead's church is one of the older foundations in Cowal. It was mentioned in 15th century records, and contains an elaborate late 16th century memorial to the Campbells of Ardkinglas. There are many stones of interest in the older part of the graveyard, including, on a fenced obelisk, a seriously OTT eulogy to a 19th century Campbell of Drimsynie which contrasts markedly with the simplicity of his wife's inscription.

Windthrow: The shallow roots of conifers give poor support against a full gale if the soil is saturated and soft, as it often is here with our annual rainfall of around 2500 mm (about 100"). Look between points 19 and 20.

0   METRES   1000

Approximate Scale

© Crown Copyright

SECTION 6

LOCHGOILHEAD - ARDGARTAN
10.1km (6.3 miles)

Route Details

Distance	10.1km (6.3 miles)
Degree of Difficulty	Moderate to Strenuous
Ascent	540m (1770ft)
Time	6 hours

Start and Finish Points

Start: Lochgoilhead PO at GR 200012. Buses: see Section 5.
Finish: Ardgartan T.I.O. at GR 269037 (Tel. 01301 702432).
Buses: Garelochhead Minibuses (01436 810200) & Citilink coaches (08705 505050). Trains: Glasgow/Oban/Fort William from Arrochar Station (6km). Large Forestry Commission Caravan & Campsite + shop nearby (GR 274031, Tel. 01301 702293).
Hotels & B&Bs + other services in Arrochar village (5km).

Maps Needed

OS Pathfinder No. 368 (NN 20/30)
OS Landranger No. 56

Parking Facilities

Lochgoilhead: at GR 199012 (PO)
Ardgartan: by Tourist Information Office at GR 269036

Route Description

■ **1** Start outside Lochgoilhead PO. Facing the loch, take the nearest road (of 3) to your R. It leads inland for 100m, past the public toilets and other buildings before giving way (L bend) to a path which disappears into a tunnel of trees & bushes. Emerge to cross a stile (with gate) and continue uphill to a forest road at GR 202013 (250m from start).
■ **2** Turn neither L nor R. Instead, above L, a rougher track leads up past a gate to pass R of a conifer wood. Go through the gate (50m), or over its two neighbouring stiles, to follow the track uphill for 1km to another gate and stile. (Trees L, open hill R all the way).
■ **3** Continue into the forest on the track for 400m (level), until it drops to a footbridge. Cross it.
■ **4** Ignore path L Ahead a path is signed ('Coilessan Hill Path'). Follow it, steeply at first, then curving R to continue more gently. The path is obvious. After 650m, pass large boulders and soon afterwards (50m) emerge into the foot of a wide ride leading up R (a sign points back to 'Lochgoilhead').
■ **5** Follow the ride uphill past a white marker post. A burn runs to your L. The path is a 'trod' now, but clear. The ride bends L: continue up to a junction with another ride (230m).
■ **6** Ignore L turn ('Glen Croe'), but continue up (signed 'Coilessan'). Near its top, the ride bends R (boggy) and leads directly to a stile in the forest fence.
■ **7** Cross the stile (awkward).

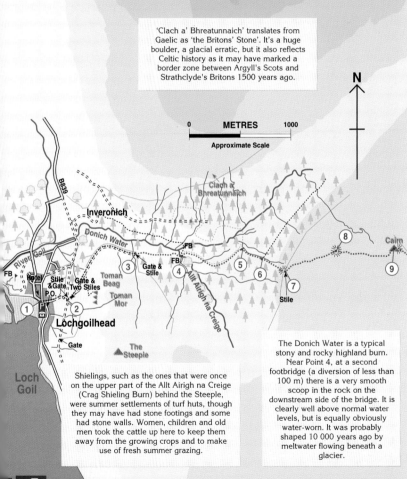

© Crown Copyright

'Clach a' Bhreatunnaich' translates from Gaelic as 'the Britons' Stone'. It's a huge boulder, a glacial erratic, but it also reflects Celtic history as it may have marked a border zone between Argyll's Scots and Strathclyde's Britons 1500 years ago.

N

0   **METRES**   1000
Approximate Scale

Clach a' Bhreatunnaich

Inveronich

Donich Water

B839

River Goil

FB

Hotel

Stile & Gate
P.O.

Gate & Two Stiles

3   Gate & Stile

4   FB

Toman Beag

Toman Mor

5

6

7   Stile

8

9   Cairn

1

2

Lochgoilhead

Gate

The Steeple

Loch Goil

Allt Airigh na Creige

Shielings, such as the ones that were once on the upper part of the Allt Airigh na Creige (Crag Shieling Burn) behind the Steeple, were summer settlements of turf huts, though they may have had stone footings and some had stone walls. Women, children and old men took the cattle up here to keep them away from the growing crops and to make use of fresh summer grazing.

The Donich Water is a typical stony and rocky highland burn. Near Point 4, at a second footbridge (a diversion of less than 100 m) there is a very smooth scoop in the rock on the downstream side of the bridge. It is clearly well above normal water levels, but is equally obviously water-worn. It was probably shaped 10 000 years ago by meltwater flowing beneath a glacier.

There are waymarker posts across the open hill between here and the forest top in Coilessan Glen and in clear weather you simply follow them. BUT CARE: the path reaches 500m, so cloud is a real possibility. You may need to navigate accurately with map & compass if the posts cannot be seen. There is a trodden path, but it is often faint and the line not obvious. Climb steeply (up & L: 120m vertically, 600m horizontally, several markers) to the top of the slope (post on knoll). If needed, the direct mag. bearing to Point 8 from the stile is 74° for 600m. It will take you R of the early posts. Since the line rises obliquely L across the slope, beware of drifting down too far L.

■ **8** In clear weather, the posts curving R, then back L to Point 9 (cairn on small knoll, 550m away) are all visible from here across the broad pass. The faint 'trod' goes slightly uphill, levels, then drops before a last rise to the knoll & cairn. The downhill section is particularly faint on the ground. The mag. bearing from Point 8 to 9 is 91° for 550m: if going this way you'll descend immediately to cross boggy flats before the final rise to the knoll & cairn.

■ **9** The cairn overlooks Coilessan Glen. Below it a grassy basin drops steeply E to the forest top (mag. bearing 103° for 230m to Point 10). If clear, three posts can be seen leading down through the basin (R of a burn and fence in its lower part) to a gate & stile in the forest fence 20m R of a fence junction. Path traces are very faint at first.

■ **10** Through the gate is the start of a good ATV path. Follow it very steeply down through the forest (2 footbridges) to a junction with a forest road (600m).

Folded schists on the Steeple, Lochgoilhead

■ **11** Turn R on the (dirt) road. Follow it down to a fork (850m).

■ **12** Take the R fork for 450m to a junction beyond a concrete bridge.

■ **13** Ignore R turn. Go straight on for 650m to a T-junction.

■ **14** Turn L Go 200m to cross a concrete bridge. Road now tarred. Follow the tarmac surface down for 1km to a gate.

■ **15** Ignore R turn at gate, but continue on the tarmac road to ....

■ **16** .... Ardgartan Tourist Information Office at GR 269037 (2.1km; end of Section 6). Pass a Caravan Club site. Unless heading for the Forestry Commission's Ardgartan camp site (shop) or the youth hostel, ignore the R turn for them (signed) at 1.7km from the gate and also all other minor turns.

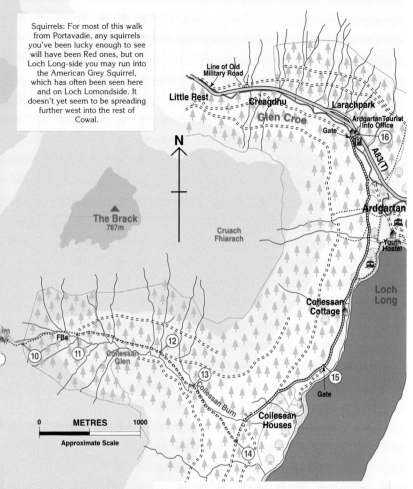

Squirrels: For most of this walk from Portavadie, any squirrels you've been lucky enough to see will have been Red ones, but on Loch Long-side you may run into the American Grey Squirrel, which has often been seen here and on Loch Lomondside. It doesn't yet seem to be spreading further west into the rest of Cowal.

Line of Old Military Road

Little Rest

Creagdhu

Glen Croe

Larachpark

Ardgartan Tourist Info Office

Gate

(16)

A 83 (T)

N

The Brack
787m

Cruach Fhiarach

Ardgartan

Youth Hostel

Loch Long

Coilessan Cottage

(10) **(11)** FBs

Coilessan Glen

(12)

(13)

Coilessan Burn

(15)

Gate

| 0 | METRES | 1000 |

Approximate Scale

Coilessan Houses

(14)

Gaelic is not much spoken in Cowal to-day, but most local place names are at least partly in that language. Lochgoilhead is a mixture; Ceannlochgobhal - anglicized as Kinlochgoil - is the Gaelic ('ceann' meaning head and 'gobhal' a fork or angle). To-day you're crossing Ardgoil (='The Heights in the Fork?' - between Lochs Goil and Long?) to Coilessan, which is almost pure Gaelic for 'Wood of Waterfalls', and then going on to Loch Long, which is both Gaelic and Norse (= 'Loch of the Ships').

6

Summary of the Loop Walks

■ **Walk 1 Portavadie and Low Stillaig.** This is a beautiful corner of Cowal, mostly open moorland, with wide sea views to sharp peaks on the island of Arran and across Loch Fyne to Kintyre. If you're here on a day of restricted views, you can make the most of the coastal detail around the beaches of Port Leathan and Salann Bay and the rocky shores of Eilean Aoidhe. There's a lot for the imagination, too. Though not spectacular, the minimal outline marking where the chapel once stood, together with its wide surroundings, is capable of stirring wonder at the sheer scale of the task that faced Columba's spiritual heirs. The outward route has some slow going, but persevere; the rewards are good and the return, though uphill, easy.

■ **Walk 2 Tighnabruaich - Kilfinan.** and return. This walk has its origins in an old coach road between the two villages, though the line through the forest isn't exactly as it was. The original route is followed between Kilfinan and Acharossan, and at the southern end, but elsewhere it traverses forest rides along slightly different lines. These forests bring their own particular rewards; there is a great peace and quiet, the real possibility of coming across a small group of deer and

the joy of an occasional sudden widening of horizons, especially if you divert a little to climb Cnoc Uaine or its SW top. There is also plenty of shelter in bad weather (though underfoot things can be wet) and, along the Stowhall Burn, there are lovely stretches of birch woodland. At Kilfinan, the church's Lamont aisle has a fascinating collection of early christian and medieval carved stones. Transport arrangements to return to Tighnabruaich, if required, are best confirmed beforehand, preferably the previous day.

■ **Walk 3 Glendaruel (Bealachandrain).** Easy going throughout, though often steep, on forest roads and the very quiet public road that crosses the high Bealachandrain pass. It features great views over Glendaruel, and glimpses into the depths of wooded gorges. The road by Bealachandrain is one of the earliest non-military modern roads in the highlands, having certainly been in existence in 1769, when it was re-aligned. It formed part of the main east-west route through Cowal between Dunoon and mid-Argyll, crossing Loch Fyne at Otter Ferry where the elegant former ferry-house and quay still stand, the former now a pub / restaurant.

■ **Walk 4 Loch Eck Forest.** Entirely on forest road, except for one short but easily-crossed break where a landslip removed the track a few years ago! There are many breaks in the trees, allowing frequent grand views over narrow, beautiful Loch Eck to the rugged mountains above its east shore. Contrast with these steep mountains is provided right at the start in the gentle green fields of the strath floor by Glenshellish Farm. From about 1830, David Napier, who owned Glenshellish, established a steamer service along Loch Eck, connected at either end with Strachur and Kilmun by steam-driven carriages.

■ **Walk 5 Ben Donich Circular Tour.** After a steep start, reward comes in a gentle kilometre of path leading to a lovely corner by the Donich Water, where mature trees surround waterfalls on a rocky burn. From here the passage through the upper glen, drawn on by glimpses of the Cobbler's sharp peaks, is on paths and forest rides until wild open country is reached in the approaches to the Bealach Dubh-lic pass. Having crossed the bealach (pass) and gained a forest road, the underfoot going is easy for the rest of the day. The last climb to the head of Glen Croe and the subsequent descent towards Lochgoilhead through Gleann Mor is enlivened by views to surrounding craggy mountains, a line of waterfalls and an oakwood.

■ **Walk 6 The Cobbler.** Superlatives are appropriate for this most dramatically rocky of mountain tops. A great day out in its own right, or, if you've crossed Cowal from Portavadie, a fitting climax to your tour, with wide and wonderful views. But it's definitely a tougher day than others in this book; a real mountain walk, needing some experience. You could be in trouble if cloud comes in and you can't use a map and compass. There is a trodden path all the way to the summit, but it's not waymarked, and you could lose it high up if you're very careless. If you choose the ridge route down over An t-Sron (prolonged excellent views) as opposed to reversing your route up, remember that, in poor visibility, it demands good navigation. Either way, save some energy for the last steep descent to the finish. A hard day, but one offering great rewards and a sense of achievement.

■ **Walk 7 Glen Loin and Coiregrogain.** A great route for exploring and admiring the Arrochar mountains without actually having to climb them! Coiregrogain (the name for a ruined house but also for the glen to its west) runs deep amongst the highest and most rugged of these hills, being surrounded by four 'Munros'. No less dramatic is rocky Binnein na Circe; a spur of A'Chrois that looms over the ruined house. Do take some time just to stand and stare. Underfoot going is good; our approach beside Glen Loin's woodlands is along track and made path, the ascent into Coiregrogain is along quiet road and track servicing a hydro-electric scheme and our return back around the lowest slopes of A'Chrois is all on forest road.

PORTAVADIE AND LOW STILLAIG
5km (3.1 miles)

Route Details

Distance	5km (3.1 miles)
Degree of Difficulty	Moderate
Ascent	130m (430ft)
Time	3 hours

Start and Finish Point

Portavadie; the road junction NE of Pollphail village at GR 932691.

Maps Needed

OS Pathfinder No. 413 (NR 86/96)
OS Landranger No. 62

Parking Facilities

Portavadie at GR 928698. With consideration for local residents, roadside space may also be found near the start/finish point.

Route Description

■ **1** Begin at GR 932691, the entrance to deserted Pollphail village. A Rights of Way Soc. sign points L of the village outside its boundary fence. De facto, everyone takes the concrete road L of the housing blocks for 200m to their far L corner, where a 'trod' rises through the broken fence beyond a ditch to rejoin the official line.

■ **2** Go up the trod, rising obliquely R through birches, to the top of a broad heathery ridge.

■ **3** Path disappears. Head S on the higher ground for nearly 300m (dip then rise; views). (Part way on, faint sheep trods low down to R provide an easier alternative). Eventually two standing stones can be seen ahead, slightly R (0.6m & 3.0m tall; the taller one leans NW - R as you see it).

■ **4** Go down (or continue low on R) to stones (GR 931683; 200m).

■ **5** From the stones, follow broad, high ground SW (300m) to a heathery top (or pass to its L).

■ **6** From the low top, look for Low Stillaig (ruin), 300m S. Go L of the ruin towards the shore at Port Leathan (much bracken lower down, use sheep trods). Past the ruin, bear R to pass L of a good house and reach Port Leathan c.300m from its head,

■ **7** Walk L to an isthmus (300m).
(If time, explore Eilean Aoidhe).

■ **8** Go to a Boys' Brigade outdoor centre (obvious, 100m). Follow a track inland from here for 450m N past a standing stone (on L).

■ **9** Follow the track for 1500m more to the public road (tarmac) at GR 942690.

■ **10** Turn L here, and follow the road for 1km back to the start.

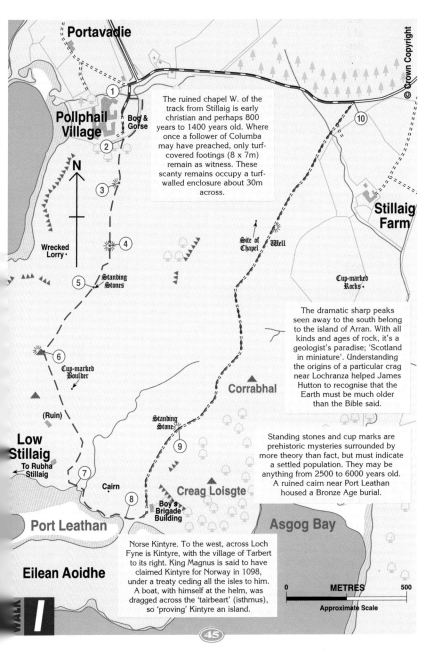

Portavadie

① **Pollphail Village**

Bog & Gorse

②

③

N

④

Wrecked Lorry •

⑤ Standing Stones

⑥

Cup-marked Boulder

(Ruin)

Low Stillaig

To Rubha Stillaig

⑦

Port Leathan

Cairn

⑧

Boy's Brigade Building

Eilean Aoidhe

⑩

Stillaig Farm

Site of Chapel   Well

Cup-marked Rocks •

Corrabhal

Standing Stone

⑨

Creag Loisgte

Asgog Bay

© Crown Copyright

The ruined chapel W. of the track from Stillaig is early christian and perhaps 800 years to 1400 years old. Where once a follower of Columba may have preached, only turf-covered footings (8 x 7m) remain as witness. These scanty remains occupy a turf-walled enclosure about 30m across.

The dramatic sharp peaks seen away to the south belong to the island of Arran. With all kinds and ages of rock, it's a geologist's paradise; 'Scotland in miniature'. Understanding the origins of a particular crag near Lochranza helped James Hutton to recognise that the Earth must be much older than the Bible said.

Standing stones and cup marks are prehistoric mysteries surrounded by more theory than fact, but must indicate a settled population. They may be anything from 2500 to 6000 years old. A ruined cairn near Port Leathan housed a Bronze Age burial.

Norse Kintyre. To the west, across Loch Fyne is Kintyre, with the village of Tarbert to its right. King Magnus is said to have claimed Kintyre for Norway in 1098, under a treaty ceding all the isles to him. A boat, with himself at the helm, was dragged across the 'tairbeart' (isthmus), so 'proving' Kintyre an island.

0   METRES   500

Approximate Scale

WALK **1**

LOOP WALK 2

TIGHNABRUAICH - KILFINAN AND RETURN
16.6km (10.4 miles)

Route Details

Distance	16.6km (10.4 miles)
Degree of Difficulty	Moderate
Ascent	460m (1520ft)
Time	7 hours

Start and Finish Points

Tighnabruaich at GR 977728 (A8003 / track junction, between a large stone villa (L) and a white house ('Tregortha', R)). (to Kilfinan Hotel GR 934789; this is an 'out and back' route, not a true loop). Transport contacts? - see p.12

Maps Needed

OS Pathfinder No. 400 (NR 87/97)
OS Landranger No. 62

Parking Facilities

Tighnabruaich at GR 983731.
Kilfinan village nr. hotel or church.

Route Description

■ **1** Go up the track past 2 ruins on L. Near 3rd ruin (200m) take path on L (sign for Kilfinan). Gorse. Iron gate (400m), then into dense woodland via a boggy clearing. Ford Allt Mor in 100m.

(post). Climb 1.1km till path flattens. Ignore ride fork (L), to bend L (post) into clearing (2km total).

■ **2** Go round clearing's R edge (post; path not obvious) into first forest ride on R. Follow it NW 500m (boggy, then clearer path) to a fence & ride coming from L.

■ **3** Follow the fence on its R, uphill, to a corner. Leave it R, to a cragfoot (climb hill above for view?). Go L along cragfoot, then descend ride, L, to a forest road (400m; signs at road).

■ **4** Turn R on road for 100m (to sign to forest ride on L: 'Kilfinan').

■ **5** Take ride NW; rise past a wall to a forested watershed (900m). Continue gently down, NW, along the ride, (often open on R) to a ruined stone wall in 350m.

■ **6** Continue, ignoring branching rides. Reach R bank of Stowhall Burn; follow down till path crosses burn (500m).

■ **7** Follow the ride, NW, down to a small clearing; birches/ride lead R to Stowhall Burn (ignore).

■ **8** Continue NW to ride end. Posts lead L to wood edge & wall.

■ **9** Follow the wall R, 50m, then go L between burn and a fence / wall. Stile. On to gate and track.

■ **10** Cross bridge; track to farm buildings; bend R. Go 400m to gate, & 300m more to two gates.

■ **11** Stay on old track (ignore R turn). Pass more gates to reach the B8000 at GR 931782

■ **12** Turn R, 800m downhill to...

■ **13** ...Kilfinan church and hotel. Return by the outward route or arrange transport.

46

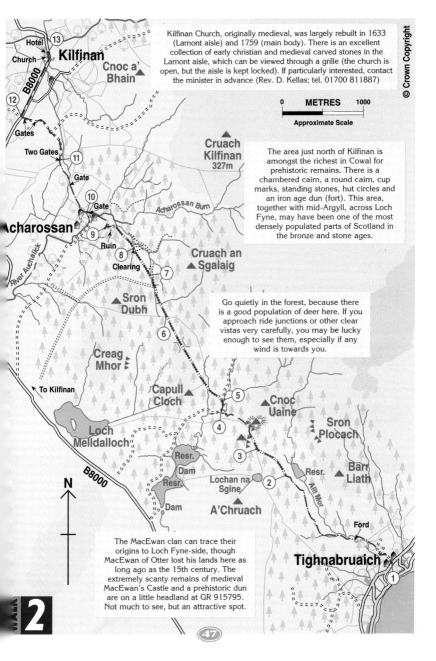

Kilfinan Church, originally medieval, was largely rebuilt in 1633 (Lamont aisle) and 1759 (main body). There is an excellent collection of early christian and medieval carved stones in the Lamont aisle, which can be viewed through a grille (the church is open, but the aisle is kept locked). If particularly interested, contact the minister in advance (Rev. D. Kellas; tel. 01700 811887)

© Crown Copyright

Kilfinan

Hotel (13)
Church ✝
Cnoc a' Bhain ▲

B8000

(12)
Gates
Two Gates (11)
Gate (10)
Gate

0   METRES   1000
Approximate Scale

Cruach Kilfinan ▲
327m

The area just north of Kilfinan is amongst the richest in Cowal for prehistoric remains. There is a chambered cairn, a round cairn, cup marks, standing stones, hut circles and an iron age dun (fort). This area, together with mid-Argyll, across Loch Fyne, may have been one of the most densely populated parts of Scotland in the bronze and stone ages.

charossan

(9)
Ruin (8)
Clearing (7)

Acharossan Burn

Cruach an Sgalaig ▲

Sron Dubh ▲

River Auchalick

(6)

Go quietly in the forest, because there is a good population of deer here. If you approach ride junctions or other clear vistas very carefully, you may be lucky enough to see them, especially if any wind is towards you.

Creag Mhor ▲

← To Kilfinan

Capull Cloch

(5)
Cnoc Uaine ▲
Sron Plocach ▲

(4)

Loch Meldalloch

Resr.
Dam
Resr.
Dam

(3)
Lochan na Sgine (2)
A'Chruach ▲
Resr.
Barr Liath ▲

B8000

Alt Mor

Ford

N
↑

The MacEwan clan can trace their origins to Loch Fyne-side, though MacEwan of Otter lost his lands here as long ago as the 15th century. The extremely scanty remains of medieval MacEwan's Castle and a prehistoric dun are on a little headland at GR 915795. Not much to see, but an attractive spot.

Tighnabruaich

(1)

3

GLENDARUEL (BEALACHANDRAIN)
8.9km (5.4 miles)

Route Details

Distance	8.9km (5.4 miles)
Degree of Difficulty	Easy
Ascent	340m (1120ft)
Time	3.5 hours

Start and Finish Point

A8003 / forest road junction at GR 998823 300m S of Waulkmill

Maps Needed

OS Pathfinder No. 388 (NR 88/98)
OS Landranger No. 55

Parking Facilities

A little, by the forest road entrance.

Route Description

■ **1** Go up the forest road, crossing under electricity lines twice (450m).

■ **2** Continue uphill for 600m beyond the lines to a viewpoint N over Clachan of Glendaruel.

■ **3** Continue climbing for another 1.5km on the steep, twisting track to reach an excellent viewpoint along Glendaruel from a road bend above a gorge.

■ **4** Continue up to the road summit (500m) then descend about 300m to cross the Cam Allt (= crooked burn; 'cam' = bent, and occurs in the names Cameron and Campbell; 'sron'=nose & 'beul'=mouth). A little less than 100m beyond the burn, having rounded a L-hand bend, look for a junction, where an older track goes R at 90°.

■ **5** Turn R onto the older track, (wet, with rushes) to follow it, at first gently downhill, but then up for more than one km., to reach the public road beyond a gate and electricity lines and near the summit of the Bealachandrain pass (1.8km from the junction).

■ **6** Turn R and descend towards Glendaruel. After just over 1.5km of bends, come to 500m of fairly straight road, beyond which (all downhill) a view opens out over Bealachandrain Farm and the lower part of Glendaruel.

■ **7** Continuing, the road descends a hairpin bend, then curves L past Bealachandrain Farm to reach a disused junction (safety barrier R) 100m beyond another L bend (1km).

■ **8** Turn R at the barrier to cross a partly collapsed stone bridge with care. (The alternative is to go via the A886 and A8003). Follow the disused road SE for 600m to its junction with the A8003 at Waulkmill.

■ **9** Go R on the A8003 for 300m to regain the start.

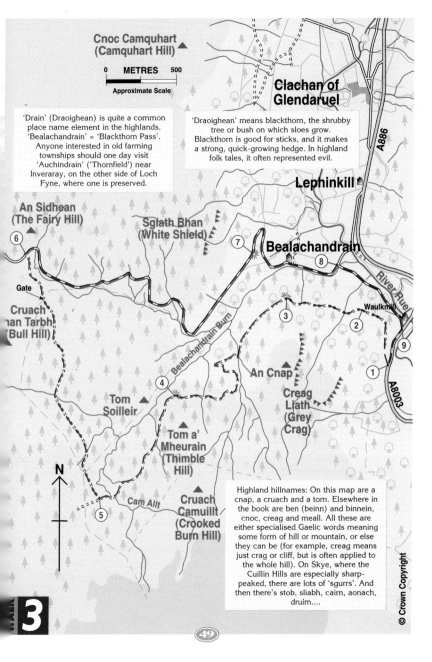

Cnoc Camquhart
(Camquhart Hill) ▲

0   METRES   500
Approximate Scale

Clachan of
Glendaruel

'Drain' (Draoighean) is quite a common place name element in the highlands. 'Bealachandrain' = 'Blackthorn Pass'. Anyone interested in old farming townships should one day visit 'Auchindrain' ('Thornfield') near Inveraray, on the other side of Loch Fyne, where one is preserved.

'Draoighean' means blackthorn, the shrubby tree or bush on which sloes grow. Blackthorn is good for sticks, and it makes a strong, quick-growing hedge. In highland folk tales, it often represented evil.

Lephinkill

A886

An Sidhean
(The Fairy Hill) ▲

Sgiath Bhan
(White Shield)

⑥

⑦

Bealachandrain

⑧

River Ruel

Gate

Cruach
an Tarbh
(Bull Hill)

③

②

Waulkmill

⑨

①

An Cnap ▲

Creag
Liath
(Grey
Crag)

④

A8003

Bealachandrain Burn

Tom
Soilleir ▲

Tom a'
Mheurain ▲
(Thimble
Hill)

N

⑤

Cam Allt

Cruach
Camuilt ▲
(Crooked
Burn Hill)

Highland hillnames: On this map are a cnap, a cruach and a tom. Elsewhere in the book are ben (beinn) and binnein, cnoc, creag and meall. All these are either specialised Gaelic words meaning some form of hill or mountain, or else they can be (for example, creag means just crag or cliff, but is often applied to the whole hill). On Skye, where the Cuillin Hills are especially sharp-peaked, there are lots of 'sgurrs'. And then there's stob, sliabh, cairn, aonach, druim....

3

© Crown Copyright

LOCK ECK FOREST
15.4km (9.6 miles)

Route Details

Distance	15.4km (9.6 miles)
Degree of Difficulty	Easy
Ascent	390m (1280ft)
Time	5 hours

Start and Finish Point

Bridge at road junction GR 111972 (sign; Glenshellish Farm)

Maps Needed

OS Pathfinder No. 379 (NS 09/19)
OS Landranger No. 56

Parking Facilities

Glenbranter: at GR 111977 (Lauder Forest Walks).

Route Description

■ **1** Cross the bridge to E and fork immediately L in front of Glenshellish Farm. Follow this track for 2.1 km to a junction by the head of Loch Eck. The flat, wet flood plain to your L at the head of the loch shows pioneering woodland species spreading over 'new' alluvial ground deposited by the river

Cur. Fast-growing, many-seeded willow and birch predominate, with some wet-loving alder. The river meanders widely and has left an ox-bow.

■ **2** Ignore the track from the R (potential short cut), but carry on (loch to L) to a fork (1.9km).

■ **3a** Take L fork (2.6km, loch still to L) to another fork in the track.

■ **3b** Short cut to point 6 if you turn R here, instead.

■ **4** Bear R to climb away from the loch into Bernice Glen. Arrive at a junction in 1.0km. Halfway. The house at Bernice is now an annex of an Edinburgh-owned outdoor centre at Benmore, near the south end of Loch Eck.

■ **5** Turn sharply R to return high above Loch Eck, across which is the Whistlefield Inn, once the haunt of drovers. In 3.0km come to point 6 (the shortcut from point 3 joins from the R here).

■ **6** Continue straight on for 2.1km, with Loch Eck well below to your R, to where the track now ends because of a landslide (ignore, after 300m, an ATV path that rises steeply L off the track).

■ **7** Cross the old landslide easily to continue on the mossy line of the track for 400m to a junction.

■ **8** A new track link comes up from the R (point 2); ignore. Continue ahead for 1.8km to a junction (views over Glenbranter).

■ **9** Turn downhill to the R (ignoring a L turn in 200m) to the foot of the slope (450m). The bridge at point 1 is just to your L.

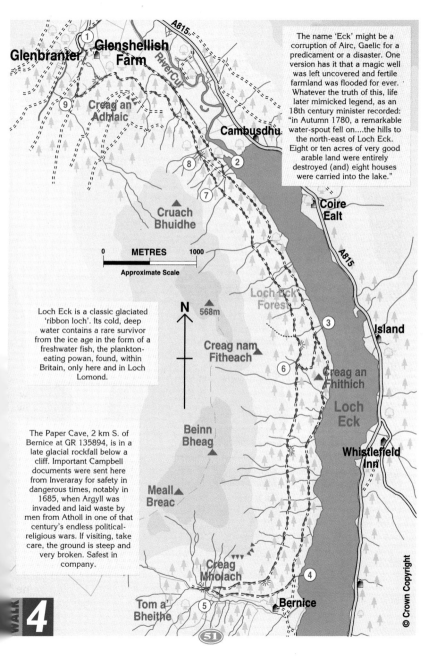

Glenbranter

Glenshellish Farm

A815

River Cur

① ⑨

Creag an Adhlaic

Cambusdhu ②

⑧ ⑦

Cruach Bhuidhe

Coire Ealt

A815

0 METRES 1000

Approximate Scale

Loch Eck Forest

Loch Eck is a classic glaciated 'ribbon loch'. Its cold, deep water contains a rare survivor from the ice age in the form of a freshwater fish, the plankton-eating powan, found, within Britain, only here and in Loch Lomond.

N

568m ▲

Creag nam Fitheach

③

Island

⑥

Creag an Fhithich

Loch Eck

The Paper Cave, 2 km S. of Bernice at GR 135894, is in a late glacial rockfall below a cliff. Important Campbell documents were sent here from Inveraray for safety in dangerous times, notably in 1685, when Argyll was invaded and laid waste by men from Atholl in one of that century's endless political-religious wars. If visiting, take care, the ground is steep and very broken. Safest in company.

Beinn Bheag ▲

Whistlefield Inn

Meall Breac ▲

Creag Mholach

⑤

Bernice

Tom a' Bheithe

④

(51)

© Crown Copyright

WALK 4

LOOP WALK

5

BEN DONICH
CIRCULAR TOUR
16.3km (10.2 miles)

Route Detail

Distance	16.3km (10.2 miles)
Degree of Difficulty	Strenuous
Ascent	560m (1840ft)
Time	7 hours

Start and Finish Point

Inveronich (tracks junction) at GR 203021 (E of houses and barn).

Maps Needed

Either OS Pathfinder Nos. 368 (NN 20/30) (mainly) & 367 (NN 00/10) or Harvey's 'Arrochar Alps'.
OS Landranger No. 56

Parking Facilities

Inveronich at GR 203021(above)

Route Description

■ **1** From the car park, a track runs gently uphill into trees. After 50m or so, turn L on a path which climbs steeply to 130m before relenting. Views. 1km on it drops steeply to cross two footbridges 100m apart, the second at GR 213017.
■ **2** Turn L here (don't cross second bridge) and follow a good path ('Coilessan Hill Path') for 650m to a wide ride and a sign pointing back ('Lochgoilhead').
■ **3** Turn uphill, R. The ride bends L (white post) and rises by a burn to a ride junction (230m).
■ **4** Turn L ('Glen Croe'), into a contouring ride. Follow it for 1.6km, crossing small burns, till it dips to meet the meandering main burn (GR 231029).
■ **5** Cross the burn, go R, then away from the burn to exit from the forest (fence & white post, 500m).
■ **6** A faint line goes to the head of the glen, keeping L of and a little higher than the pass at its head, to pass L of a knoll and overlook Glen Croe opposite the Cobbler (GR 240042; 1.2km).
■ **7** Follow the path down to cross a forest fence (stile). Continue down the path to a forest road.
■ **8** Turn L, 1.7km, to a junction.
■ **9** Turn L to the head of Glen Croe (track junction; 850m)
■ **10** Turn L (W) on a forest road into Gleann Mor. Go for 5.1km to a track junction near the public road at a cottage (GR 193042).
■ **11** Turn sharp L for 1.2 km. (ignore a track, late on L) to join the public road at GR 198037.
■ **12** Turn L on the B839 for 1.4km. to a 90° R hand bend.
■ **13** Go straight on (track) for 200m (ignore gated track on L) to a track junction.
■ **14** Turn L for 100 m, and go R of a large black barn to the start / finish car park (GR 203021).

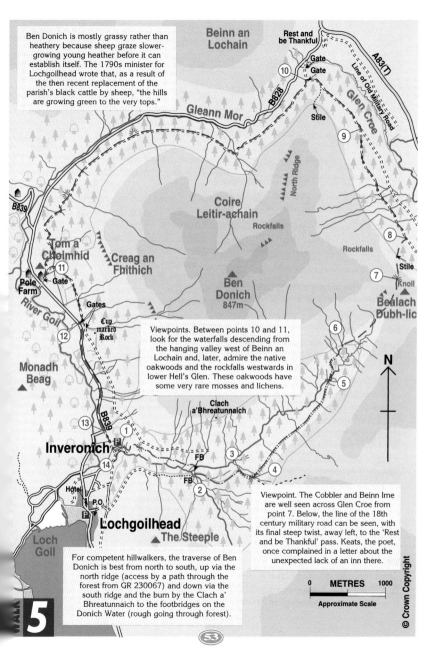

Beinn an
Lochain

Rest and
be Thankful

Ben Donich is mostly grassy rather than
heathery because sheep graze slower-
growing young heather before it can
establish itself. The 1790s minister for
Lochgoilhead wrote that, as a result of
the then recent replacement of the
parish's black cattle by sheep, "the hills
are growing green to the very tops."

A83(T)

Gate

Line of Old Military Road

Gate

⑩

B828

Glen Croe

Gleann Mor

Stile

⑨

North Ridge

B839

Coire
Leitir-achain

Rockfalls

⑧

Stile

Tom a'
Choimhid

Rockfalls

⑦

Creag an
Fhithich

⑪

Knoll

Gate

Ben
Donich
847m

Bealach
Dubh-lic

Pole
Farm

Gates

River Goil

⑫

Cup
marked
Rock

⑥

Viewpoints. Between points 10 and 11,
look for the waterfalls descending from
the hanging valley west of Beinn an
Lochain and, later, admire the native
oakwoods and the rockfalls westwards in
lower Hell's Glen. These oakwoods have
some very rare mosses and lichens.

⑤

N

Monadh
Beag

Clach
a'Bhreatunnaich

⑬

B839

①

Inveronich

P

FB

③

⑭

④

FB

②

Hotel

P.O.

Viewpoint. The Cobbler and Beinn Ime
are well seen across Glen Croe from
point 7. Below, the line of the 18th
century military road can be seen, with
its final steep twist, away left, to the 'Rest
and be Thankful' pass. Keats, the poet,
once complained in a letter about the
unexpected lack of an inn there.

P

Lochgoilhead

The Steeple

Loch
Goil

For competent hillwalkers, the traverse of Ben
Donich is best from north to south, up via the
north ridge (access by a path through the
forest from GR 230067) and down via the
south ridge and the burn by the Clach a'
Bhreatunnaich to the footbridges on the
Donich Water (rough going through forest).

© Crown Copyright

0   METRES   1000

Approximate Scale

5

53

6

THE COBBLER
9.0km (5.6 miles)

Route Detail

Distance	9.0km (5.6 miles)
Degree of Difficulty	Extremely Strenuous
Ascent	910m (2990ft)
Time	7 hours

Start and Finish Point

Car Park by Loch Long (A83 / Succoth road jnct; GR 294048).

Maps Needed

OS Pathfinder No. 413 (NN 20/30)
or Outdoor Leisure 39 or Harvey's 'Arrochar Alps'.
OS Landranger No. 56

Parking Facilities

As above (start) or in Arrochar.

Route Description

■ **1** Cross the A83 from the car park. A little L, a path leads L into trees for <100m to a R bend, then rises, straight, steep & rough, for 1km (cross a forest road on way).
■ **2** Turn L along a level path for 1km to a junction above a dam.
■ **3** Take the path's R fork above the dam and up the glen, past the

Narnain Boulders, to where it crosses the main burn (1.3 km).
■ **4** Cross the burn (care). The path rises boggily R, crosses a smaller burn & passes R of a large crag to become steep, stony and broken, but so well trodden that its line is clear to see. Climb steeply below the N Peak to the main col on the ridge at GR 261060 (0.9km; 320m above the main burn). N Peak rises R.
■ **5** Turn L for the highest top (Centre Peak). The path crosses boulders, then rises back to the ridge. A little R is the true top, a finger of rock needing some rock climbing ability; most simply admire it from a nearby 'top'. Bad visibility? Descend by route up.
■ **6** If not: Face the main top. Go down R below it, then by a rocky ridge for 150m to the narrowest part below the S peak's cliffs.
■ **7** Zig zag down R off the ridge, moving 50m+ away from the S Peak, to descend parallel to & R of it on a grassy band until below its lowest rocks (drop 120m in 250m). Move L to regain the ridge at a broad col (GR 263055).
■ **8** Turn R to climb a knoll SE of the col (<20m in 100m). Continue SE down the broad ridge crest ('trod'). Descend a steep face, cross a broad col and climb a second top (An t-Sron, GR 268052; 700m from 8). Continue 700m more along the ridge to its end above Loch Long.
■ **9** Return 30m to the last dip. A 'trod' drops E (via a little gully) to the dam (GR 280051, 600m).
■ **10** Cross the burn to point 3.

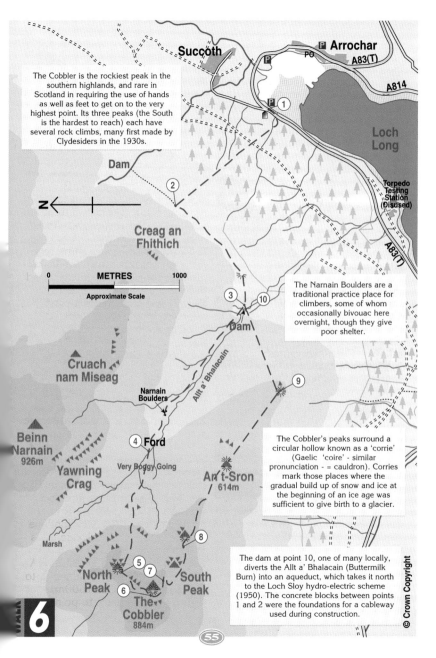

The Cobbler is the rockiest peak in the southern highlands, and rare in Scotland in requiring the use of hands as well as feet to get on to the very highest point. Its three peaks (the South is the hardest to reach) each have several rock climbs, many first made by Clydesiders in the 1930s.

Succoth

Arrochar

PO

A83(T)

A814

Loch Long

P ①

Torpedo Testing Station (Disused)

A83(T)

Dam

②

N ←

Creag an Fhithich

③ ⑩

Dam

The Narnain Boulders are a traditional practice place for climbers, some of whom occasionally bivouac here overnight, though they give poor shelter.

| 0 | METRES | 1000 |

Approximate Scale

Cruach nam Miseag

⑨

Narnain Boulders

Allt a' Bhalacain

Beinn Narnain 926m

Yawning Crag

④ **Ford**

Very Boggy Going

An t-Sron 614m

The Cobbler's peaks surround a circular hollow known as a 'corrie' (Gaelic 'coire' - similar pronunciation - = cauldron). Corries mark those places where the gradual build up of snow and ice at the beginning of an ice age was sufficient to give birth to a glacier.

Marsh

⑧

⑤ ⑦

North Peak

⑥

South Peak

The Cobbler 884m

The dam at point 10, one of many locally, diverts the Allt a' Bhalacain (Buttermilk Burn) into an aqueduct, which takes it north to the Loch Sloy hydro-electric scheme (1950). The concrete blocks between points 1 and 2 were the foundations for a cableway used during construction.

© Crown Copyright

6

7

GLEN LOIN AND COIREGROGAIN
15.4km (9.6 miles)

Route Details

Distance	15.4km (9.6 miles)
Degree of Difficulty	Moderate to Strenuous
Ascent	360m (1180ft)
Time	6.5 hours

Start and Finish Point

Car Park at the head of Loch Long; W of river, by A83/ Succoth road junction (GR 294048).

Maps Needed

OS Pathfinder No. 413 (NN 20/30)
or Outdoor Leisure 39 or Harvey's 'Arrochar Alps'.
OS Landranger No. 56

Parking Facilities

As above (start) or in Arrochar.

Route Description

■ **1** Turn R out of the car park to follow the A83 across Loin Water bridge (400m).
■ **2** Turn L beyond the bridge, to follow a track (river to the L) past Stronafyne Farm (450m). Continue N on the track along the E side of Glen Loin to GR

308072, where it becomes a well-made path (2km) (=2.5km from the A83).
■ **3** Follow the obvious path N through the forest ride, alongside the pylons, climbing, at first, past a viewpoint, then levelling out to cross a flat section, beyond which a narrower ride leads away L into the trees just before the wide ride drops to the Inveruglas Water (1.7km).
■ **4** The path goes through the narrower ride (600m) then drops R to reach the Inveruglas Water at a bridge (100m).
■ **5** Cross bridge; go 100m to a junction (tarred road). Go L along it for 600m to a junction.
■ **6** Turn L (straight on is for Sloy Dam) and follow a track over a bridge and up into Coiregrogain glen for 3.1km. Pass a quarry [1.8 km], then a dam (R) at GR 279089 to reach a junction, near a second dam, at GR 275083.
■ **7** Turn L to cross the Allt Coiregrogain (burn) below the 2nd dam. Rise R a little, before turning sharply back L to follow a track E, back down the S side of Coiregrogain. Follow this track for 5.6km (no significant junctions) to where it crosses the Allt Sugach Burn at GR 293055 (250m past an area of younger trees with a view of the village).
■ **8** Descend the L bank of Allt Sugach on a rough path (cross a track) for 350m to a tarred road.
■ **9** Turn R to follow the road for 400m back to the start.

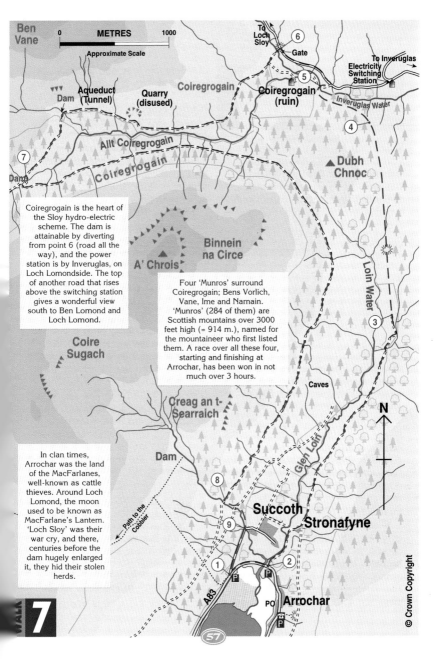

Ben Vane

0   METRES   1000
Approximate Scale

To Loch Sloy ⑥

Gate ⑤

To Inveruglas
Electricity Switching Station

Coiregrogain

Coiregrogain (ruin)

Inveruglas Water

▾▾▾ Dam   Aqueduct (Tunnel)   Quarry (disused)

Allt Coiregrogain

Coiregrogain

⑦
Dam

④

▲ Dubh Chnoc

Coiregrogain is the heart of the Sloy hydro-electric scheme. The dam is attainable by diverting from point 6 (road all the way), and the power station is by Inveruglas, on Loch Lomondside. The top of another road that rises above the switching station gives a wonderful view south to Ben Lomond and Loch Lomond.

▲ Binnein na Circe

A' Chrois

Loin Water

③

Four 'Munros' surround Coiregrogain; Bens Vorlich, Vane, Ime and Narnain. 'Munros' (284 of them) are Scottish mountains over 3000 feet high (= 914 m.), named for the mountaineer who first listed them. A race over all these four, starting and finishing at Arrochar, has been won in not much over 3 hours.

Coire Sugach

Caves

Creag an t-Searraich

N

In clan times, Arrochar was the land of the MacFarlanes, well-known as cattle thieves. Around Loch Lomond, the moon used to be known as MacFarlane's Lantern. 'Loch Sloy' was their war cry, and there, centuries before the dam hugely enlarged it, they hid their stolen herds.

Dam

⑧

Path to the Cobbler

⑨

Glen Loin

Succoth

Stronafyne

① ②

P   P

A83

PO   Arrochar

P

57

Heritage of the Area

■ Section 1

Portavadie to Tighnabruaich

Glenan Forest Nature Reserve (near Point 1) Car Park at GR 928698 The Forestry Commission's broadleaved woodland at Glenan is a good example of native west-highland oakwood. As well as the dominant oaks, other tree species include birch, hazel, alder, rowan, ash, willow, wych elm, gean, aspen and holly. Designated an FNR in 1988, it includes a good succession of vegetation from the shore, through the woodland, right up to open heath. Nightjars breed here in June / July. May is good for woodland flowers such as wood sorrel, wood anemone, celandine, violet and bluebells, and also to avoid high bracken, though the woods are accessible at all seasons by paths starting from the car park.

Asgog Castle (Point 7) GR 946705 A junior branch of the Lamont clan built this now ivy-covered, ruinous tower house in the mid-15th century to consolidate their hold on SW Cowal.

When Campbells besieged the (royalist) Lamonts in 1646, the defenders were eventually ordered by their clan chief to surrender, along with those from Toward. Having surrendered, both castles were burnt and, despite guarantees of safety, 36 leading Lamonts were hanged at Dunoon. Many followers were simply dirked or buried alive.

Kames Powder Works, Millhouse (Points 10 - 11) Low Mills centres on GR 958705 Local charcoal and water (for both power and process) brought gunpowder manufacture here in 1839. Despite several accidents down the years, powder was made until 1921.

The Low Mills, in woodland S of the village street, contain upwards of 20 ruined process buildings and mills, together with a cooperage, the largest building near the entrance. Safety features included building-separation, massive walls (roofs were deliberately weak) and trees to baffle blast. The brick cottages opposite, on the Kames road, were for workers; on the manager's gable, a circular space once held the works' clock. In a field at GR 956707 is a powder tester - a small cannon - in which is forever rusted a standard ball, designed to go a standard distance if the powder was good. At GR 963709, well away from the village, are the massive walls of the magazine. Ask locally about access to these sites.

Kames Crossroads (Point 17) GR 971714 At the crossroads, in a hedge opposite a shop, are two standing stones, perhaps 4000 years old! There is a third by the war memorial.

The Kyles & Shinty (between Points 17 & 18) GR 973716 A pitch below the road is home to

Kyles Athletic who play shinty, a sport unique to highland Scotland. With a small, hard ball and sticks a bit like hockey sticks (but without hockey's restrictions on how to swing them), head and hand injuries are always a risk in this hard-fought game. Kyles are one of the country's top teams.

■ **Section 2**
Tighnabruaich to Glendaruel
Tighnabruaich (centred on Point 1) GR 979728 Tighnabruaich's many beautiful villas and gardens were designed for mid-19th century 'merchant princes'. The pier was built in 1843, and from then on Glasgow people and Glasgow money poured in. Other piers, now disused, followed at Kames (1856) and Auchenlochan (1879), and a ribbon of villas sprang up, as they did everywhere around the Clyde that was accessible by steamship or train.

As you pass through, look for excellent, often delicate, examples of ironwork, occasional stained glass, and frontages featuring dormer windows and gables. And don't forget the gardens, with their Victorian attachment to rhododendrons and 'monkey puzzle' trees. Frank Arneil Walker, in his excellent 'Argyll and Bute' volume of 'The Buildings of Scotland' series is especially taken with William Leiper's Tighnabruaich House; "a grand residence....Arts and Crafts with a hard edge".
Caladh Harbour (Points 6 & 7)

GR 004757 The Victorian Gothic of Caladh Castle, SW of the harbour, was demolished in 1959, but plenty of the estate's contemporary landscaping remains.
Ormidale (between Points 11 & 13) Ormidale is probably a Norse name meaning 'Serpent Valley', and refers to lower Glendaruel. While there are adders in Cowal, they are very rarely seen and 'serpent' here refers to the rearing curved prows of the viking longships that once sheltered in Loch Riddon. The name survives at Ormidale House (at GR 002817) and Ormidale Lodge, also known as Craig Lodge (at point 11).
Glendaruel: Bealachandrain Bridge (near Point 14) GR 995831 According to W H Murray, the name Glendaruel is a Gaelic play on words. It may come from 'Gleann na ruith-fhuil' meaning 'Glen of Bloody Water', replacing the original 'Gleann na ruadh-thuil' ('Glen of Red Water') following a battle between Scots and Norsemen fought, perhaps near Bealachandrain, in 1110. Defeated, the slaughtered Norwegians were dumped in the river, hence the 'bloody water'.
Bealachandrain Farmhouse (near Point 14) GR 991831, with its adjacent enclosed court, is typical of many such farm steadings built by landowners (here Campbell of Ormidale) in the late 18th or early 19th centuries. Highland lairds, following the social upheavals consequent on the failure of the Jacobite cause, were converting

their estates from near subsistence economies with densely-populated farming townships into cash-based regimes pursuing the new scientific agriculture on large farm units.

■ Section 3

Glendaruel

Clachan of Glendaruel (Point 1) GR 996842 Glendaruel is old. The hillside east of the Clachan has cup-and-ring-mark rock carvings and a stone age chambered burial cairn as well as post holes, hearths and pottery from the huts of stone age farmers. The glen may be the setting for the old Irish story of Deirdre, Naoise and the sons of Uisneach.

Kilmodan Church (in the Clachan near Point 1) GR 995841 Kilmodan Church dates largely from 1783. It marries presbyterian simplicity with Georgian elegance. 'Kil' (cell) names represent places where early celtic saints built simple places for themselves (their 'cille') and preached the word.

In a small building in the churchyard is a fine collection of carved 14th and 15th century grave slabs, all of which once lay in the churchyard itself.

Lucknow Gate (Point 4) GR 997866 The Lucknow Gate was built, in imitation of its Indian original, by the Campbells of Glendaruel. A member of the family fought at the siege of Lucknow during the 'Indian Mutiny' of 1857.

The last Glendaruel House was built in 1900 but burned down in

1970. The Campbells had departed in 1915 and the estate has since been broken up.

Kildalvan (an abandoned farming township above Point 9) GR 017889 Kildalvan, abandoned before 1850, is on a terrace at 100m, NE of a burn. A little higher, and 250m NE, is the site of a medieval chapel (GR 018892).

Kildalvan has remains of houses, byres and a barn; a kailyard and stackyard and two corn-drying kilns. From a much earlier period, there is a boulder with a dozen prehistoric cup marks and a rock basin for husking barley.

Between the township and the chapel the ground rises and falls in old cultivation rigs. In the traditional run rig system, the patches of best ground (infield) were worked annually, the outfield was rested much more often and the bulk of the ground was shared as rough hill grazing. The tenants made joint decisions and paid a communal rent, much of it in kind.

This was little beyond subsistence farming, though cash was made through the sale of cattle to drovers. Kildalvan's way of life started to collapse with the social and economic upheavals following the 1745 Jacobite uprising.

The chapel is represented only by grassy footings, about 7m long and 5 wide. Local tradition speaks of a healing well nearby (Tobar na Suil, or 'Well of the Eyes').

Dunans Castle (near Point 12) GR 040911 Not really a castle, but a mansion in the 19th century Scots baronial style following the fashion set at Balmoral. It has recently (Jan 2001) suffered a major fire.

■ Section 4
Glendaruel - Glenbranter
Commercial Forests (Most Points)
Much of to-day's walk is on Forestry Commission land and, except for the hilltops, is mostly planted with non-native conifers (the only conifers native to the British Isles are scots pine, yew and juniper).

Here in the west, the single most commonly-planted species is sitka spruce, from the north-western seaboard of North America. Sitka grows very quickly in mild, moist Argyll; its needles are short and sharp and the foliage as a whole looks blue-ish.

Other commonly-planted species include european and japanese larch and their hybrid. These are the conifers that shed their needles each autumn, so they provide much-needed colour then, and when fresh in spring. Recognize them in summer by the rosette arrangement of each group of needles (except at twig tips).

The commercial forest earns cash and provides and supports jobs from land that has restricted potential (though the Commission's workforce has declined in recent decades). Long-term it can also improve the quality of peaty soils. Opponents cite the relatively poor, fast-growing timber our mild climate produces, the dull appearance of monoculture conifers relative to native broadleaf woodland and the poverty of associated species.

Deer in the Forest (eg Points 9-10) Red deer are associated in our minds with open hill, but they're thought to have evolved as a woodland species and numbers are rising, partly through the spread of conifer plantations. The advantage in shelter is obvious, but there is also food. Grass grows in rides and clearings, beneath larch, and at the forest edge. Sharp needles are palatable young, and so is the bark of some species (willow and rowan, which pop up in odd places even amongst the conifers, are favoured).

Because of dense cover, though, you may see nothing. Instead you must look for signs such as these: footprints (cloven hoofed, bigger than sheep prints); bushy, mis-shapen trees and broken stems where new growth has been nibbled; scars and tooth marks on the trunks of younger trees where strips of bark have been torn off; more ragged scars where new-grown antlers have thrashed a bush to knock away decaying 'velvet'; low 'tunnels' where pathways enter thick vegetation; droppings; clumps of hair (browny-red, straight and stiff); black, peaty wallows where deer roll, and, finally, cast antlers, though these are often eaten to short stubs to replenish scarce calcium.

■ Section 5
Glenbranter - Lochgoilhead
Strachur village and vicinity (W of Point 2) GR 0901 Strachur church (GR 095015) dates from 1789. Medieval grave slabs are set in its walls. Near the door is a gravestone to McPhunn of Drip, who, being cut down too early, survived his hanging (for sheep stealing) at Inveraray and lived to a good age as 'half-hung Archie'. The former inn, opposite, is from the 1790's.

The building of church and inn were financed by General John Campbell, who fought and grew wealthy in America. During the 1780s he built Strachur House (GR 091016). To-day, walkers are welcome in the eastern and northern ends of its park, away from the house, on paths near to the Inverglen Burn (access from near the church). At Strachur Smiddy, (GR 096013, open afternoons), a leaflet gives information on these paths.

The 'Fairy Knowe'; a dome-shaped hilltop at GR 070977 (visible on the SW skyline from Point 3) Sidhean Sluaigh (= 'the fairy hill of the multitude') is a typical highland 'fairy hill' - steeply rounded and distinctive. An 18th century minister wrote: "melodious music was frequently heard, and gleams of light seen in dark nights." Many traditional tales relate people's disappearance in such circumstances. Fairies were mischievous!

Laird's House site (GR 123016;
near Point 5) and Roy's Map Strachur House's predecessor was here, but no trace remains. It was marked on General Roy's military map of the 1750s, the first detailed topographical map of all the highlands and a forerunner of the Ordnance Survey.

The woodland mapped by Roy is similar in extent to to-day's native broadleaves (only 2% of Argyll), showing that forest clearance had already been achieved.

Rockfalls above the Curra Lochan (Points 13-14) GR 1600 The tumbled masses of rock high on the hillside are the result of 10000-year-old landslides.

During the ice age, the glacier that eroded this glen scraped away so much of the flank of Beinn Lochan that, when the ice-support melted away, the hillside collapsed. Such landslips, around which are many stories of ambush, plunder and refuge, provide excellent shelter for foxes and (rarely) wildcats.

Iron Bloomeries (near Point 18) GR 170996 At the Lettermay Burn crossing, look for chunks of iron slag on the stream-bed (mostly smooth, with gas holes, grey in colour and very heavy). This is the waste from a bloomery - a small, charcoal-fired clay furnace of the type that once provided the remoter highland blacksmith with his supply of iron, produced at the rate of about a fist-sized piece daily.

The raw material for such bloomeries was a thin, toughened layer of soil called iron pan.

■ Section 6
Lochgoilhead - Ardgartan
The Donich Water Walk, Argyll Forest Park and the new Loch Lomond National Park (Point 4)
GR 213018 The Donich Water walk at point 4 is maintained by the Forestry Commission, which designated much of north Cowal as the 'Argyll Forest Park' as long ago as the 1930s.

Scotland's first National Park is soon to be established around Loch Lomond and the Trossachs, and, though the core area doesn't extend west of Loch Long, the Forest Park may yet be included. It would be appropriate, as there is a long and strong tradition of the leisure use of land here, complementing farming and forestry.

A Natural Landscape? (Point 8)
GR 228018 The image many have of the Scottish highlands is of naturally bare hill and moor - heathery, rocky, and wild. Without human management, though, they would have looked very different. For 6000 years people have been farming in Scotland and to do it (and for other reasons) they have cleared woodland. The long-term effect has been to remove natural woodland from all except 2% of the highlands.

Once cleared, the grazing and browsing of cattle, sheep and deer (especially since the extinction of the wolf) is very effective in preventing re-generation. Often the only trees on an otherwise bare hill grow in gullies or gorges or on rocks where they were inaccessible when young.

So this landscape, though magnificent, is rarely natural, except, perhaps, in gorges and on the highest tops above 600 or 700 m, where conditions are severe. Even on the hilltops, the trampling and selective grazing of sheep has subtly altered the balance of species growing there.

Loch Long ('The loch of the ships') and the Norsemen (beyond Point 15) Part of the fleet belonging to King Haakon of Norway sailed up Loch Long in 1263. Some of the smaller boats were dragged from Arrochar to Tarbet (in Gaelic, 'Tairbeart' means isthmus) to attack settlements on Loch Lomond.

The 1750 Military Road through Glen Croe (Point 16) Glen Croe was the line that army surveyors chose for their road from the garrison town of Dumbarton to Inveraray (the Duke of Argyll's 'capital'). The upper glen preserves the old road's line to the 'Rest and be Thankful' pass.

Roughly 1000 miles of military road were built in 18th century Scotland from the same motive that produced Roy's maps - fear of Stewart rebellion.

Maps and roads helped to end traditional clan society. The chiefs' feudal power, built on private armies of tenants, protected by isolation, and frequently opposed to central government, could not survive modern communications.

Walking & Safety Tips

It is absolutely essential that anyone venturing out into the countryside, particularly hilly terrain, be correctly prepared to reduce the risk of injury or fatality. No amount of advice could cover all possible situations that may arise. Therefore the following walking and safety tips are not intended to be an exhaustive list, but merely a contribution from our personal experiences for your consideration.

Clothing & Equipment

The lists represent the basic equipment required to enjoy a full day's hill walking, reasonably safely and comfortably.

CLOTHING:- Strong, sensible footwear, preferably boots with a good sole, but strong trainers or lightweight boots can be worn during prolonged dry weather; warm shirt, fibre pile jacket, warm woollen sweater, windproof and waterproof hooded anorak and overtrousers (several thin layers insulate more adequately than one layer), thermal gloves; woollen hat or balaclava, warm trousers (avoid denim/jeans which become very clammy and cold when wet and could induce exposure), and good quality woollen socks or stockings, protected by waterproof gaiters.

EQUIPMENT:- Good compass and maps of the areas, along with a survival bag, whistle or torch for implementing the International Distress Signal - 6 long blasts/flashes in quick succession followed by one minute pause then repeated (the answering signal is 3 blasts or flashes). A basic first-aid kit should also be carried, which contains - bandages, sticking plasters, safety pins, scissors and some gauze pads. Take a rucksack in which to carry your equipment, and some food, plus extra food for emergency rations - chocolate, fruit cake, cheese and dried fruit. Extra liquid should be carried in hot weather.

Preparation & Procedure

Ensure that yourself and the others are adequately equipped and that no-one is overburdened. Learn how to use your map and compass competently. You should always be able to at least locate yourself on a map. Find out the weather forecasts for the area. Always consider the wind chill factor - even the gentlest of winds can reduce effective temperatures to a dangerous level. Plan both the route and possible escape routes beforehand, balancing terrain, weather forecast and the hours of daylight against experience whilst allowing for a safety margin. Always try to plan your walk so the prevailing wind is behind you. Always try to walk in company. It is safer and more enjoyable. Gain a basic understanding of first aid. Try to leave written details of your route, point of departure, number in your group, destination and estimated time of return. In an emergency this information could save a life. Maintain a steady rhythm, at the pace of the slowest walker. Take care when you are walking to avoid sprains. Be very careful where you step and remain extremely vigilant about avoiding the adder, Britain's native poisonous snake. Take regular breaks - mainly to check your progress and the next stage. Keep an eye on the weather. Always be prepared to turn back if necessary. On completion of your journey, inform the person with whom you left your written information of your safe arrival.

Stay Wise - Stay Alive

First aid on the hills requires both knowledge and common sense. If in doubt concentrate on the comfort and morale of the casualty. **IN AN EMERGENCY: STOP AND THINK - DO NOT PANIC.** If you are lost - check your surroundings carefully and try and locate yourself on your map. Find shelter and decide whether it is safe or best to use an escape route. If someone is injured, or is showing the signs of exposure (i.e. stumbling and slurred speech, shivering, irrational behaviour or collapse and unconsciousness) **STOP IMMEDIATELY**, prevent further heat loss, find shelter and place the casualty into a survival bag with extra clothing. Huddle together as a group and give the casualty some warm food and drink. **DO NOT**: rub the casualty, give alcohol, allow further exposure. Decide then on your next course of action. Do you go for help? or do you stay put overnight sending out the International Distress Signal? If you have to stay put overnight try and find or make adequate shelter, conserve food and drink, keep morale high, keep the casualty warm, dry and conscious, and use the International Distress Signal. If you are able to leave someone with the casualty whilst two of your party go for help from a village or farm the following information is essential; accurate location of the casualty, nature of injuries, number injured, number in group, condition of others in group (if one person is suffering it is possible that others will be too), treatment already given, and time of accident. Remember that **WET + COLD = EXPOSURE**. This rapid cooling of the inner body can lead to fatalities. **ALWAYS BE PREPARED.**

How to Use this Guide

This guide is designed to be used by walkers who have some experience, are appropriately dressed and equipped, and are able to interpret Ordnance Survey Maps.

■ **1** CHOOSE YOUR ROUTE Study the map of Cowal on pages 10 & 11 indicating the locations of the 13 walks, then consult the individual route summaries, route descriptions and route maps before making your personal choice. Each 'loop' walk starts and finishes at the same point for your convenience (but check notes for loop walk 2).

■ **2** CHECK THE ROUTE SUITABILITY Carefully study your selected route to ensure that it is suitable for you, but particularly for the weakest member of your party. To do this also consider the grading system for the length and degree of difficulty of each route (contents pages) - as well as the detail in each individual walk description.

■ **3** CHECK THE WEATHER CONDITIONS Before you set out it is essential that you check the current and developing weather conditions. In addition, you should consider the Walking and Safety Tips on pages 64 and 65. Also be aware of the telephone numbers of the emergency services.

■ **4** USE WITH AN ORDNANCE SURVEY MAP This guide is designed to be used with the relevant 1:25 000 and 1:50 000 scale O.S. Maps of the area should you so wish. Grid references are used in the guide.

■ **5** USING THE MAP AND ROUTE DESCRIPTION TOGETHER This guide is designed so that the route map and route description can be easily used together. The detailed, concise route descriptions are clearly numbered in both the text and on the route map to help you locate your position.

The Cobbler from the south east